Failing, Fabulously!

Love After Marriage

Keri Ross

Copyright © 2019 by Keri Ross
ISBN: 978-1-09-238612-8
www.keriross.com

For my bury-the-body buddy, Karen…

While not the fodder for this story, our friendship and escapades became the foundation for a fabulous and zany life!

Acknowledgements:

I am blessed to have had the influence and assistance of those who helped me check "write a novel" off the bucket list and who are influential in this fabulous journey:

My forever friends – Karen, Alex, Jill, Darla, Teresa, Tammy, Sheri, Susan, Keri, Luke, Ladena, Cathy, Lupe, Linda, Paula, Brenda, Donna, Tina, Steve, Harold, Rehnee, Richard, and John – what a fabulous village!

Specifically:
Alex, for the enduring and unconditional friendship and many travels;
Teresa, for lighting the fire and giving me feedback;
Darla, for trying to keep me on track…in every way;
Tammy, for reframing my pain and introducing me to your brother;
All my Central Office co-workers, for listening, laughing, and loving me through my darkest times;
Steve, for banishing me to the library and igniting my love for reading and writing;
Dorothy, Jason, and Rose for the publishing tips;
The Bookless Club, for the laughs and support and for agreeing to actually read this book;
Jillian, for your wisdom; Jacob, for your honesty; and Hali, for your advice;
Jase and Emery, for the distractions and the joy;
Dad and Mom, for never failing me;
My entire extended family, for the love and moments that matter;
And John, for the belief that soul mates really do exist and the prospect of the sublime.

Further, I am blessed by my Heavenly father who gifted me the rings of Saturn and the Marfa lights on back-to-back nights in West Texas, and who made available to all eternal life through Jesus Christ, His son.

...And just for grins:

Keanu Reeves, for portraying the archetypical bad ass and making my world much more aesthetically pleasing;
Sam Elliot, for sharing your deep, sensuous, toe-curling voice;
Malcom Gladwell, for imparting poignant social insight;
Diana Gabaldon, for exquisite storytelling and taking the time to hear my story and write a cherished inscription;
Elizabeth Gilbert, for sharing your story, the one that resonated on the beach and helped me find True North;

And finally, to all US Veterans, for your service and sacrifice because one should never pass up the chance to thank a Veteran.

Prologue:
It's a Legitimate Question

How do you meet someone? That was my question. After thirty years of marriage, my husband went through the stereotypical middle-aged rite of passage, otherwise known as a midlife crisis. He quit the job, bought the sports car, and had the affair. I was too busy to notice until it was too late to fix. I was in the crux of my career, and thinking I had his devotion and support, was barreling forward with intense focus and unbridled hours towards the next promotion.

The promotion came as the marriage spiraled out of control. Progressively, I had moved, literally and figuratively, from the bedroom to the couch to the guest room. Finally, I filed for divorce and moved out of the house - exactly two days before turning the BIG 5-0.

Needing a quick and clean break and somehow feeling guilty because I didn't want to live with my cheating ex-husband anymore, I took very little: a few plastic tubs of my personal stuff, clothes and shoes, a dining room table that belonged to my parents, and a loveseat I had picked out specifically for my home office a decade ago.

A decade ago and a few weeks later, I discovered that the office would have to be converted to a nursery. Unexpectedly pregnant at 40 turned out to be par for the course for big life changes surrounding both my 40th and 50th birthdays!

But I digress because two days before the tidal

wave of 50 washed over me, I sat alone on the floor in an unfamiliar, too large, almost empty three-bedroom house looking at six plastic tubs that seemed to hold the sum total of my five decades of life. I put my head in my hands and had the much-deserved pity party cry.

My son was grown and married and had his first child just a few months before. I can remember the look on my soon-to-be ex-husband's face as he found out five days after he bought the sports car that he was going to be a grandpa. It was quite a blow to all the effort he was putting into recapturing his youth. As for me, I couldn't be more excited at the prospect of becoming "Gigi" and having a little rug rat to love and spoil.

My son met his wife in college and never really came back home after his senior year. Although I had his blessing to end the marriage, his love and support were a two-hour drive away. It was Saturday, and the ex and I had decided since my new house was sans furniture, my daughter would spend that first weekend (of her not-so-ideal future of alternating weekends) with her dad, primarily because he stayed in the family home, and all of her stuff was there. Not to mention his house (no longer *our* house) had beds!

I spent the next year hanging out with friends. My three very close girlfriends from the office got me through the most difficult times. The four of us seemed to each personify a stereotype and collectively form some sort of synergistic unit. Teresa is quiet and silently wise when it comes to almost anything, but especially, when it comes to something earthy and natural. For instance, if you are allergic to poison ivy, she knows just the remedy – chew on a leaf or two and build up an immunity. She is one of the most beautiful people in the room, but instead of being conceited or aloof, she bestows her radiance on everyone else. You can't be around her for even a few minutes without a little of her splendor rubbing off on you.

Darla is gifted with spiritual insight and conflict resolution. She can look at any situation and instantly drill down to the heart of the matter and address the root of the problem. She is a parent liaison charged with settling disputes before they are brought to administration. The outcome of her work usually reaches much further, helping parents understand their children, helping children take responsibility for their actions, and causing everyone a little self-examination and spiritual growth.

Tammy is worldly, well-read, and well-traveled. She exudes culture, art, and style; and she is eternally optimistic. She doesn't allow her friends to wallow in self-pity or even hard-earned misery; instead, she deftly reframes the situation to show you how good things really are. I am the audacious and intellectual one who seems to have more misadventures than adventures. I'm never afraid to try something new, and I've always got a story to tell.

The truth is, we all four share bits and pieces of all of these traits – wisdom, beauty, spirituality, positivity, and intellect – and it was our commonalities more than our differences that caused us to bond. Tammy was the one who introduced us all to the idea of seeing everything from the perspective of "fabulous" – and it was a great perspective to adopt. Why in the world should you simply tell your girlfriend her new hairdo is cute when you can tell her it is absolutely fabulous? And there's nothing like the way a girl with a slow Texas drawl can say "fabulous"! You have to drag it out so that the first vowel is almost pronounced twice and each syllable somehow gets accented: *fa-a-bu-lous*! Can you imagine working in an environment with this collective positivity? I was blessed.

It was Darla and few other friends who surprised me on my dreaded fiftieth birthday by dragging my puffy red eyes and tear-stained cheeks to a Japanese steakhouse complete with a sashimi-wielding chef who playfully shot risqué jokes at the party and squirted sake in our mouths as he conjured Americanized washoku before our eyes. She also lent me her couch until my mother came to visit, dragged my sad tail end (her words) to the store, and forced me to buy furniture to fill the house.

My trio of friends – Darla, Teresa, and Tammy – distracted me, prayed for me, encouraged me, laughed with me, and mostly reminded me how much better off I was each day to be on my own and away from the Narcissistic asshole, which is mostly how we referred to my ex.

My best guy friend, Alex, was a lifesaver as well. At first, the weekends when I did not have my daughter were unimaginably painful. I grieved the shift from full-time to part-time parent. It was unnatural for my nine-year-old to be away from me half the time. I had agreed to a 50-50 shared custody arrangement because my young daughter with the old soul was insistent on fairness and spending equal time with both parents. I wanted her to feel the least amount of guilt, pain, or regret possible; so in my own guilt, pain, and regret did what I thought was best for her.

It was killing me! Alex who had divorced three years earlier and basically "lost" the nearly-grown stepchildren he had raised knew better than most the muck I was wallowing in. He would have none of it and made a point to spend every other weekend distracting me with one adventure after another. So gradually, the worst experience of my life faded, I adopted the new normal, and somehow started discovering who I was as a single, independent adult. Eventually, I was ready to date, which brings me back to the original question: How do you meet someone?

This was a legitimate question. I live in a small town, worked at the same school district for twenty years, went to a small church. I knew almost everyone in my limited circle, and there was no single, divorced, or widowed dashingly handsome and successful man my age in that circle I'd even consider going out with. I didn't participate in the bar scene, barely even drank fruity light-weight concoctions, and I hadn't dated anyone other than the Narcissist in thirty-three years.

Let's think about that for just a minute. The last time I went on a first date, I was in my teens and had all the necessary requirements for confidence in dating: *Teen Beat* magazine, the high-school smorgasbord of drooling boys, tiny waist accompanied by perky boobs, and limited frontal lobe function! Thirty years later I had a two-baby body, read legal bulletins and pedagogy publications for fun, and had a fully-functioning, mastered-degreed frontal lobe. None of which seemed conducive to dating. Further, most of the teenaged boys on the aforementioned smorgasbord had rings on their fingers and were scattered and busy building careers and families. So I turned to what seemed the most logical and effective way I knew of to meet men: online dating.

Part 1: Life After Marriage

1
It Might Lead to Dancing

Confident I was ready for this new chapter in my life, I began the search for what was surely destined to be a fabulous adventure in dating that would undoubtedly lead to a quick and painless connection with my yet unrevealed but patiently-waiting, perfect soul mate...or I began a slightly different journey.

Like every other decent-looking, fairly successful, financially independent middle-aged woman, I assumed this would be a piece of cake. I would just approach dating like I did my job – do the necessary research, create an action plan, implement, review regularly, and adjust as necessary.

Step one: familiarize myself with the various dating site options and choose the one best for me. This took all of ten seconds. (Okay, I skipped the research part and decided on gut instinct. I did, however, read Aziz Ansari's book *Modern Romance*, which carries online dating as its primary content. Thorough enough? I mean a book written by a comedian has to have more social integrity and truth than some scholarly research project on the subject. Right?)

My gut said, "You're a Christian woman. Obviously, it would be a bonus to find a man who is likeminded and has similar values. There is a dating site dedicated to this very philosophy. This is a no-brainer, Keri."

Now, if you've never been on a dating website, which I had not at this point, you might not know they vary quite a bit. Some require you to answer a lot of questions about yourself, and the site actually has an algorithm that will supposedly match you with like-minded individuals. On most sites, you create a profile where you describe yourself to potential dating candidates who will, in theory, read the profile and decide if they are interested in who you are as a person. Some sites, however, only require basically a screen name and a picture or two, and potential suitors just choose someone based on attractiveness. This takes the "he looks like a nice guy" to a whole new level. I don't want to get ahead of myself, but I will give you a spoiler: I have discovered I have no idea what a nice guy looks like.

So, the Christian dating venue I chose is in hindsight a middle-of-the-road type of site. It is a mixture of pics, questions, and a self-created profile where the users are in control of the searching and choosing. Anticipating quick success, I uploaded four or five of my best recent photos. By the way, becoming acquainted with online dating goes hand-in-hand with the art of taking the perfect selfie. Since my tour of duty in online dating began, I have become certain I can now pass any standardized competency exam in this area – including lighting, angles, chin tilting, posturing, duck-facing, winking, and any other area dedicated to flattering, flirtatious self-compositional photos.

Back to the dating site, I answered some questions along the lines of I prefer dogs to cats, Mexican food is the bomb, and my ideal date is strolling hand-in-hand on a beach while watching a beautiful sunset. (I mean who isn't going to love me at this juncture alone?) Then I set out to write the profile – that short essay that will definitively reach first the eyes and then the heart or maybe the very soul of that one man who is destined to find me and sweep me off my feet. I took on this task with the same diligence I approached every college essay I had ever written and was quite proud of the final product:

> *I am a born-again believer who relies on God's grace and mercy daily. I am a mom with a grown son who is married and who has his own child, and I have a preteen daughter who lives with me. I am looking for a best friend with the potential to develop into a more serious relationship if we click and God leads it.*
>
> *I want to take things slowly and develop a solid relationship based on mutual interests and core values, but there has to be a little zing from the get-go – mutual attraction, chemistry, spark, whatever you want to call it.*
>
> *Most of these profiles seem structured around dichotomy, so please rest assured I have both jeans and the little black dress in my wardrobe and feel comfortable wearing either; I can go out or stay home, don tennis shoes or high heels, bring home the bacon or fry it up in a pan – you get the picture. (And if you get the Enjoli perfume reference, we just might have more compatibility than you know.)*
>
> *I am intelligent and like to read, but it's one of many interests. I like to go to movies, dance around the house, and get out and enjoy nature. Also, I love football and would really like a man who is at least an armchair athlete. Back to the dichotomy, I certainly*

> would enjoy curling up on the sofa to watch the Cowboys, but please take me to the stadium every now and then. I don't care what team you root for, just don't hate me for my choices!
>
> In a man, strength is very important to me – mental strength, emotional strength, physical strength, and strength of character. When you put your arms around me, I want to feel that you could crush me yet know that you never would, that your strength is to my benefit. Just being honest, but I like a man to be a man.
>
> We might as well address my weakness before you send that smile – I am a thinker and sometimes that means an over-thinker. I need someone who is willing to communicate with me and talk about things of substance. I like for gestures to have meaning, and I want a man who is willing to get to know me on every level. I also have a sense of humor and want a man who can laugh at a good joke, laugh at me, and laugh at himself. Finally, I'm not looking for the perfect man; I'm looking for that imperfect man who is perfect for me.

I was especially proud of the allusion to *Enjoli*, which would undoubtedly appeal to an astute man of similar age with a sense of humor who had watched at least a little television in the '80s. I was clueless! As comprehensive as the profile was, I forgot to include, "I'm really naïve when it comes to writing online dating profiles, especially if I think anyone will read past the first paragraph or that anyone who might read further isn't yawning or running for the hills."

Here's what I thought my profile said: nice woman, good values, flexible, confident, funny, and active. Actually, my friend Alex would set me straight later (after, shall we say, a few unsuccessful weeks at making a connection). Once he stopped laughing and composed himself, he told me what my profile actually said to the average male: religious fanatic, prude, high-maintenance, critical, overly chatty, boring, and scary.

I was completely shocked by Alex's critique of my profile and had to revisit the whole "Men are from Mars; Women are from Venus" thing. One of my personal maxims had always been a William Blake quote, "You never know what is enough unless you know what is more than enough." According to Alex, I had reached more than enough a long time ago.

Alex knows me very well, and he knew I was not the lady that men would interpret, or misinterpret, from my very own words. Let me set the record straight. I love God, but I'm about the farthest thing from "religious" as you can get.

For me, faith is an integral part of who I am, but organized, legalistic religion is not. My faith means I love Jesus and I love people; it doesn't mean I'll be in church every Sunday or that I don't sin. In fact, just like most of us, I have my pet sins that I alternate entertaining and repenting!

Also, I'm not a prude. In fact, I'm fun; I laugh a lot; I tell jokes! Actually, I feel like I need to tell a joke right now (and since I grew up Baptist, I can tell this joke).

Do you know why Baptists don't believe in having sex in an upright position?

It might lead to dancing.

If you're scratching your head, as I kid, I wasn't supposed to dance because it was against the tenets of the Baptist church. I got around that by being a twirler. A twirler is really just someone dancing with a baton in her hands. I didn't mind holding the baton if it meant I could shake my booty. Now if you're worried about my childhood, eventually, my dad gave up on the pious path he had hoped for me and allowed me to go dancing even without a stick in my hand. However, the point is, I don't mind having sex in an upright position!

Also, I sometimes have the language of a salty pirate – or at least his sassy parrot. I love the English language, and I think at times it is necessary to find the word that best matches exactly the message you're trying to convey, even if that word or phrase is considered offensive by some. Hence, Narcissistic asshole. Don't get me wrong, as a former English teacher, I'm good with synonym usage and euphemisms, and I am aware of formal language for a formal audience, but sometimes you just have to be real.

The profile needed to be real and succinct:

Hey, there! I love God, family, and country. I have a wide variety of interests – enjoy everything from sporting activities to dining out and movies. I have a positive outlook on life, and I'm looking for someone who is ready to start a new adventure.

And real (and really short), got me a date – my first date in thirty-three years – with Curtis.

2
Parachuting and Pig Hunting

If you're not familiar with the process, it generally goes like this: You see a picture or a profile you like, and you send a wink or a smile emoji. If they like you, they send an emoji back as well. Then maybe someone sends a quick chat message or a hello. You respond back and forth a few times, exchange phone numbers, and the communication switches to texting and phone calls. Eventually, one person or the other gets bold enough to ask about meeting in person, and you set up a time and place to meet in a very public spot. Now, I'm generalizing and condensing, but you get the idea.

I got an online wink and "hello" from Curtis. (I must tell you at this point I've changed the names to protect the innocent and the guilty. However, I didn't change my name, so the guilty and the innocent alike will probably recognize their own circumstances and actions and self-identify, but that is just a chance I have to take because I can't make this stuff up any better than what it really is. Alex and John also gave me permission to use their real names, and because of their circumstances and influence, I felt like I had to.) So Curtis and I eventually decided to meet and settled on a popular restaurant in a neighboring town.

Now, I'm not a particularly cautious person. In fact, I'm more the meet-a-stranger-from-Craig's-List-in-a-parking-lot-alone-to-buy-a-gun kind of woman, but I decided I needed to do at least a little checking. Based on my gun-purchasing habits, you probably wouldn't be surprised to learn Curtis's "background check" was just a quick perusal on Facebook to see that he actually had an account, a variety of pictures that included him with "real" people, and a history of posts that went back more than a year.

With this information, I was thoroughly satisfied Curtis was not an axe murderer. You might be clicking your tongue at me right now, but it turns out (to this date anyway) there is zero evidence of Curtis ever murdering anyone, let alone with an axe.

So the day for the date rolled around, and I spent an exorbitant amount of time getting ready. The week before I went shopping for a new blouse. I was looking for something between Halle Berry at the Oscars and the Queen Mother on any given day. I settled for a silky button-up I could match with my best pair of two-baby-body-flattering jeans, and undid one button more than I would have for work. Complete with a pair of heels, fresh make-up, and pampered hair, I mustered my confidence and headed for the restaurant.

When I arrived, I couldn't spot anyone waiting to meet me – as I expected Curtis would do. I assumed (I realized at this point it was only an assumption) he would be outside the restaurant at the door, and I would easily recognize him from his photo, and we would exchange a quick hug or handshake, and he would shyly offer me a rose and politely lead me to the table where we would have excellent conversation and delicious food. This is how I pictured my first date in thirty-three years. Instead, I got the sick feeling in the pit of my stomach that I was about to be stood up.

That might have been the better option.

Ten minutes past the meeting time, I decided to phone Curtis, and I braced myself for the excuse I predicted I would hear. Instead, Curtis asks, "Where are you?"

It turned out he was waiting inside at a table in the bar, and I was supposed to come inside to meet him. Regrouping from my near mortification at the possibility of being stood up, I gathered up my bundle of nerves and walked through the restaurant to the bar in the back all the way to the table where I met Curtis, who was undoubtedly a few drinks ahead of me.

As I sat down, he slammed both hands on the table and almost yelled, "Keri, how the hell are ya? Do you want to go jump out of an airplane?"

What? I tried to register this question – rank it on a scale of sincerity even – and it quickly became clear he was serious. In fact, he went on to tell me he had a plane on standby. (Now, I didn't mention this before, but Curtis obviously has money and connections.)

I realized at that moment I hadn't been on a date in more than three decades, but I had no idea the new expectation for a first encounter was a death-defying leap from an airplane! My simple anticipation of looking over the dinner menu and ordering something mid-priced had not prepared me for the inquiry I was processing. I looked around the room to gather my thoughts and searched for a hidden camera. I could imagine my friends laughing as flies on the wall, but I was all alone there, so I began to explain to Curt, as he insisted I call him, that my young daughter probably needed her mom for a few more years and that possibly jumping out of an airplane was a second-date activity. He was disappointed but undaunted.

He had another surprise for me – it was a Ted Nugent bumper sticker signed by none other than Ted Nugent himself. It seems Ted and Curt are elbow bumpers and kindred spirits. Curt had just come from Ted's house, where I imagined he was probably making bullets and shooting stuff or engaging in some other equally manly endeavor, to this very destination to be with me. I knew at this point I should be more than flattered Curt left such prestigious company to meet me, but I was still trying to get over the fact that if I went out with this guy again, I would need a parachute. Something happened to me that rarely happens – I was speechless. Since my brain had blocked my mouth from forming one single coherent sentence, I began to giggle.

Curt went on to tell me how he left his second wife for NASCAR and how he likes to pig hunt on his seven-hundred acres from a helicopter and how he really likes my hair and how his family has donated buildings to a well-known university. Over the next hour, Curt revealed more and more personal facts that reassured me he was not my soul mate as I tried to get the waitress he kept sending away to take our order. Finally, she did, and we ate dinner never having left ground; however, I felt as if I've been to outer space, and I had to re-evaluate everything I thought I knew about dating. Still giggling, I searched for an out, and finally, it came. I quickly stood up, shook his hand, thanked him for the dinner and the laughs, and let him know I could find my own way back to the car.

When my friends confronted me about the date the next day, I told them this story, and by that time I have dubbed him, "Crazy Curt." However, if Curt had not been my first date in thirty-three years, and if I would have had the perspective of the online dating to come, Curt would never have earned the "Crazy" part. I just had no idea.

Now for those of you who are still wondering about shooting pigs from a helicopter, let me explain. I live in Texas, and the part of Texas I live in has a feral hog problem. In fact, it is currently estimated the feral hog population in this state alone exceeds 1.5 million. Now let me put that in perspective for you. That's a lot of breakfast sausage, or that is one feral hog for about every eighteen to nineteen people if you count the city folks; however, if you only count the people who live in the country with the hogs, it's closer to one hog for every two people. Further, the sows usually have two litters a year and each litter of piglets is usually just two shy of a dozen.

Now these wild hogs are no picnic; they do about four million dollars' worth of damage annually by destroying crops and habitat, so it is not uncommon for hunters to trap or kill them. Apparently, using a helicopter as a means to find and shoot the hogs is highly effective. Please don't think I judged Crazy Curt because he had the means and skills to imbibe in aerial depredation of feral hogs! I assure you that was not the case.

3
I Want to Put on My, My, My, My, My Stripper Shoes

After my interesting and slightly confounding date with Curtis, I got right back on the proverbial horse and was quickly asked out by another man. Now I forgot to mention most dating sites provide a bare minimum of statistics to help you make a choice for a suitable suitor. Age is almost always included and sometimes height. Weight is never asked because the developers of these sites know two truths that make it moot point: men could care less how much they weigh, and women will rarely tell the truth about what they weigh.

So my next date was with Gerald who is a year older than me and, according to his profile, about five inches taller. This is a good thing because I am known for wearing my high heels. In my previous life as a high school principal, I would daily patrol the halls with quick short steps in my stiletto-style trademark heels. Apparently, teachers and students alike could hear me tapping down the tiled hallways in their direction. It was no wonder I worked in the finest high school ever – the students were always on their best behavior, and the teachers were invariably on task and teaching up a storm.

One undesirable side effect of my high-heeled addiction was that they created fertile ground for the rumor mill. A couple of students once started a rumor I was a pole-dancer before I became a teacher. As flattering as it is that these imaginative teenagers thought my two-baby body was stripper material, it was my ability to walk adeptly two to three inches off the ground that gave credence to the narrative; and my alleged vocation of dancing on the pole elevated to nearly urban-legend status at the high school. I suppose if you can imagine a baton as a pole and twirling as dancing, then the Friday night halftime shows from my high school years were close enough. Nevertheless, I still wear high heels.

Gerald wanted to meet me at a Mexican restaurant in his home town. Yes, Mexican food – did this guy pay attention to my profile or what? Again, I went through the angst of finding the perfect outfit, another trendy blouse, snug jeans, and ankle-flattering heels. In hindsight, if you're only going to have first dates, you really only need one good outfit. I also got clarification on whether or not we would meet inside the restaurant or at the front door. I do consider all things part of the learning experience. Gerald confirmed he would meet me in the parking lot, and I anticipated this just might be a real connection.

As I drove to the location of my second date in thirty-three years, I pondered that having one less-than-ideal date before meeting that special someone was not really that big of a deal, and likely even a statistical probability. As I thought of where Gerald lived, his occupation, and even his phone voice, I decided the potential was there – right up to the moment I stepped out of the car to meet him and towered over him by several inches. That's when I learned if women fudge a little on their weight, men fudge on their height. I told myself I wasn't disappointed in his height but in the fact he lied about it. This might be the time to mention I'm a kiddie pool – although at the time I had no idea.

Being a kiddie pool was a realization that would be brought to my attention by my daughter after several years of online dating. Three years into the future, with her expansive thirteen years of experience, the little sage I loved and imparted wisdom to would exclaim, "My mother is a kiddie pool!" I immediately demanded clarification, and she was quick to point out that I didn't like this one's voice or that one's hand gestures or he wasn't tall enough or he didn't have muscles or whatever it was I didn't like about the men I had dated. She concluded, "You know, Mom, shallow, like a kiddie pool."

I was shocked. I never considered my preferences to be shallow but simply to reflect my taste in men. Since I didn't care about how much money a man earned or whether or not he was college educated or learned through the hard knocks of life, and I wasn't concerned about ethnicity or skin color, I assumed I was anything but shallow. I wrestled with this newly-found discovery. If you preferred tall to short or muscles to flab or teeth to toothless or vice versa, does that make you shallow? I had always referenced that as "my type," and now I realized my inclination to melt a little when the voice on the other end sounded somewhat like Sam Elliot with a cold was the very thing that caused my sweet, loving housemate to refer to me as a kiddie pool. In her defense, she isn't wrong.

Gerald was not only short in stature, but he had on a suit at the Mexican food restaurant that Thursday night. Granted, I was brand new to the dating scene, but I was pretty sure a chocolate brown suit and tie were outdated in most work environments, let alone on a date. Well, I might be shallow, but I'm also nice. I decided I wouldn't allow these two things to deter me from getting to know this seemingly sweet man who was buying my dinner, so I sat down and delved into conversation.

It didn't take long for me to realize Gerald and I had different end goals. I was looking for "the one." After the breakup of my marriage, I questioned whether I had ever found true love or if I had settled for the crush of a high school student who didn't know who she was. I realized my ex and I never really had much in common and didn't really enjoy each other's company that often. I knew I wanted the second time around to be different. I was looking for a soul mate, my Saturn.

4
Saturn on a Cloudy Night

On one of my adventures with my bgff (best guy friend forever), Alex, we took the winding scenic road through the Davis Mountains to the McDonald Observatory in hopes of seeing at least one planet through a telescope. I snapped pictures as sharp curves revealed slight variations of the previous vistas. Several of the observatory's telescopes sit on Locke Mountain, the darkest major observatory in the continental U.S. This location is prime not only because of the absence of artificial light and lack of atmospheric pollutants but also because of the view of the Southern sky and the number of clear nights.

However, on that day, as we traversed the path to the observatory, it had been anything but clear. Storms built and dissipated before us and there was more grey than bright blue to be seen. We both were hopeful that most of this was just typical summer thunderstorms that would disappear after nightfall. Whatever the case, we would press on and make the best of the situation. Our only chance of the trip for a Star Party – an opportunity to view planets through the telescopes – was on that night.

Before the actual Star Party, we had tickets to the Twilight Program, an informative presentation by an astronomer that would give us a quick overview of what we would hopefully be looking at in the sky later that night. As the program began, I was relieved that the presenter was not only knowledgeable but a good speaker with relaxed mannerisms as well. He began to quiz the audience about various objects in the night sky, reminiscent of "Are You Smarter Than a 5th Grader" type trivia. He talked in detail about the planets, their moons, and orbits – all of which would be significant to the viewing – if indeed there was to be a viewing. He told us about a survey in which a quarter of the people polled did not know what was at the center of our solar system. For his part, twenty-five percent of the population surveyed not knowing about the role of the sun was a sure indication of job security for astronomers.

A precocious child in the audience answered many of the questions, and I imagined some science teacher somewhere would be very proud. What was obvious, but had not occurred to me until that night, was that the planets were basically on the same plane orbiting the sun. Duh! In other words, if you could locate that line in the sky, the visible planets – Jupiter, Saturn, Venus, and Mars – would dutifully connect the dots.

We were told if we were looking at Mars that night, which apparently was not too spectacular, that would mean Jupiter or the even bigger prize, Saturn and its rings, was not visible. At 9:30 we made our way out of the Visitor's Center and up the winding path to the outdoor seating area. It was dusky dark with the exception of red ambient lighting – a color spectrum that would not interfere with viewing.

I was hopeful as I looked up at the night sky and saw stars visible in patches, but as we sat in an outdoor amphitheater and listened to the introduction and instructions of the Star Party, the clouds grew and the stars seemed fewer and fewer. The speaker told us in five or six minutes the International Space Station would cross the sky above us, and I knew he was killing a little time to wait for that event. I was even more anxious and started feeling a sense of urgency to get to the telescopes. But he talked on, and five minutes later – five minutes that seemed triple the time – several of us noticed the space station come into view. The host drew out a powerful laser and tracked it across the sky. Alex commented it was hauling ass, and I concurred it was moving fast. I breathed a little sigh of relief. At least I had seen something novel in the night sky. It would not be a total loss.

Finally, we were then told Jupiter was visible and released to go stand in line at the telescopes. Alex stopped to ask the presenter a question, and I practiced patience. Poorly. I probably need to mention that I'm not very good at waiting. Just ask God whose most frequent message to me – the message I can never quite master – is to "be still."

At last, we made our way down and took our place in the back of a long line in hopes of seeing Jupiter. We had been told the "spot" was not on the side visible to Earth, so we would only be able to see various striations of this large planet. I would take that, and as I realized how slowly the line was moving, how quickly the clouds were building, and the inevitability of Jupiter dropping below the horizon, I began to pray and ask God for a gift, "Please may I see Jupiter with my own eyes? I've traveled all this way and have only this opportunity. Your natural world always reminds me You are God. You know how much I wonder in awe at Your creation. As your daughter, may I see Jupiter?"

The line moved slowly, even stopping

completely for a few minutes as the clouds obscured the image, but gradually we moved closer to the telescope. We were about four people away when the "rest" of the family in front of us showed up to stand in line ahead of us. Ugh! More people in front of me, but they were getting glimpses of the giant planet, and I was hopeful that so would I.

I continued to practice patience and kept asking God to let me see Jupiter. To my dismay, the lady immediately ahead of me was looking through the lens when the clouds completely and finally enveloped the large planet. A few raindrops signaled the ominous. The telescopes had to be put away. The viewing was over. Headlights below us indicated many had given up and were headed out. I was deeply disappointed. I was the very next person in line, but I would not get the chance to see the giant planet. Alex and I talked briefly as we headed back to the Visitor's Center in the rainy dark. The back-up plan was more lecture and video. We were accepting of our fate and decided to hang around and learn.

This might be a good time to tell you just a little more about Alex. I met Alex in 1989 when we were both teachers at the same high school; we seemed to connect as friends immediately. I was always amused, and a little admiring, of how stubborn he was and how he always gave the administrators such a hard time about any and everything.

The problem with Alex is that he is too smart for his own good – he knows more than the average person – and it is in his nature to challenge the status quo. For example, back in the day when schools were first networking their computers and putting grades and attendance online, our district jumped on the bandwagon, hooking us up to a local area network that consisted of three neighboring schools. At a training for teachers on how to use this network, Alex pointed out it would be easy to hack. The company providing the services and the training scoffed at this and quickly dismissed his concerns.

After school that day, Alex and his frequent partner in crime – yours truly – got on a computer and hacked into the system. We were just trying to prove a point, so all we did was broadcast various "messages from Mars" that disrupted anyone who was trying to work by popping up on his or her screen every ten seconds or so.

Unbeknownst to us, our boss got a call from the network administrators that someone from his school was in the system causing problems. They sent a couple of IT guys over and did a room-to-room search. We were caught red-handed and had to fret for a weekend as to whether or not we'd have jobs the following Monday. Turns out that as long as we were willing to show them how we broke into the system, they would forgive our trespassing with few consequences. They also offered us IT jobs, but we were both enjoying our current professions too much to leave.

A completely different side to Alex's personality, however, is that he is extremely laid back and a go-with-the-flow type person when it comes to most things – like the trip to the observatory. He is also the most patient and caring man I know when it comes to babysitting a divorced friend. After milling around in the Visitor's Center for almost an hour, there was an announcement that the rain had stopped and there was some clearing. We might get another chance. Excitedly we made our way back to the telescopes and jumped in line (quickly this time) – but Jupiter had already dropped below the horizon, and it was Saturn that was visible.

And soon it was my turn. I bowed my head to the eyepiece and focused...and there it sat. A little tiny planet with rings. It was like the pictures in the book – only this wasn't a book. It took a moment for my mind to reconcile I was actually gazing upon Saturn. It was not obscure; it was not intangible; light was passing through the lens of my eye and photoreceptors were converting that information into tiny electrical images in my brain. I was perceiving the rings of Saturn with my own eyes – not a drawing, not a photograph, not a satellite image. Just me actually seeing what God had put in space. I remembered Alex and others were behind me. I didn't want to monopolize this moment and cheat someone else out of this experience, so I forced myself to walk away. I wanted to gaze again and study more, but I was thankful for the gift I had just received.

Later, as I was walking to the vehicle, I perceived God relaying a message to me, "You asked for Jupiter. I gave you Saturn. My gifts are better than your desires."

I comprehended His message to me and found immediate application in my desire to find a soul mate: I had asked God for a romantic relationship, and through the experience at the observatory, He had shown me to be still – to wait on Saturn and not settle for Jupiter. As a bonus in the meantime, He had provided me a best friend with which to hang out.

As we left that night, Alex made a poignant statement, "If we would have seen Jupiter, we would have left." He was right, and it continued to drive home the lesson: If I settle for Jupiter, I will never know Saturn. Saturn is worth the wait, and from that night on, my search for love became synonymous with a quest for Saturn.

In my opinion, Gerald wasn't looking for Saturn. He wanted a relationship to fulfill certain needs he had in his life – a mother for his young son and someone to take care of the household while he was at work. He hadn't put that on the profile. If he had, I would have never known he was a good five inches shorter than me when I was wearing heels!

5
Topless Dating

My pursuit of Saturn continued and led me to David (later known as David #1 upon meeting David #2) who would actually be the first guy that would get a second date. I met David, a professional golfer, at a Mexican restaurant as well. I had done my usual background investigation and discovered through some Facebook trolling that he had recently been playing golf in Saint Helena, California, home of Nancy Pelosi's vineyard. It was also easy to detect David's political leanings – more than just a little conservative. I had my in.

When I arrived at the restaurant, I was greeted by a tall, handsome man. We made our way to the table and engaged in the usual chit chat. Finally, he brought up that he had been golfing in Saint Helena, and I was quick to respond, "Oh, I know that place. I have an aunt who owns some property there."

He said, "Really? That's a cool coincidence."

I said, "Yeah, she's actually famous – or infamous – depending on your perspective." He became really curious at this point. I continued, "Yeah, she's a divisive person – either you love her or hate her – but I think she's great."

He wanted to know who I was talking about. "Her name is Nancy Pelosi. Have you heard of her?" I asked devilishly.

I saw his countenance drop as his hopes for a connection with me were shattered. He likely made the quick assumption that I was a liberal extremist like my "aunt." And it was obvious, he is not the type of man to waste time on a liberal extremist. I started laughing and let him off the hook. Nancy Pelosi is not related to me after all, and while I did not reveal my political preferences to him, I did divulge I'm not a fan of hers. We had a really good laugh, and he decided he liked me right away.

We discussed the things we like to do and discovered we both enjoy playing ping pong and set our second date for a pool hall nearby that just happened to have a ping pong table. The third person I've dated in thirty-three years seemed to be a charm, and I was really excited to meet with him again.

At the pool hall, it quickly became obvious David didn't like to lose, and he beat me most of the games we played. Just about the time we would get in a nice volleying rhythm, he would whack the ball with such force and speed that I was more concerned with getting out of the line of fire than returning the play. Although I got a few good zings on him every now and then, I was ultimately unimpressive against him. I rationalized that he is a professional athlete in a game that involves a ball – even if it's not a ping pong ball, it's almost the same size – and he *should* be better at this than me!

I was not at all offended that David didn't let me win, but I was a little concerned he didn't mind sending missiles in my direction. However, in spite of getting spanked in ping pong, the second date was really fun. I guess he thought so as well because he asked me if I'd go on a third date, to which I replied, "Sure, what do you want to do?"

His very serious answer was, "I don't care as

long as it involves you taking off your shirt."

WHAT? Again, I'm relatively new to this over-fifty, online dating stuff, but is it the typical expectation to get naked on the third date? And do you lay that out as a ground rule? It doesn't matter what we do, but your shirt must come off? Is four hours the limit for platonic interaction? Should I just show up not wearing a shirt at all if it just has to come off anyway?

Whether or not I would have wanted intimacy with David at some point was now beside the point. It was painfully clear to me at that moment I'm a romantic. I picture making love with someone the first time after my divorce in a much different way: a-Yanni-playing-in-the-background, sitting-at-a-pottery-wheel-with--hands-in-the-mud, you-had-me-at-hello, Joan-Wilder-and-Jack-Colton–dancing–in-Columbia-and-romancing-the-stone kind of way. At the most, David was being a cad, and at the least, he had no game. Within minutes, I made my exit.

6
Smarter Than the Average Vertebrata

At this point, I realized maybe I needed to expand my horizons beyond my first impetuous choice. In spite of the dating site's target audience of Christians, I had not really had any experience on there that set it apart as the Holy Grail of good men. I had already been lied to and hit on – not to mention I had been approached by scam artists online who just wanted to see if I had any money with which I didn't mind parting. I didn't go out with any of these men, of course, but I would be remiss not to at least mention their presence.

For those of you that have never had the pleasure of online dating, always be wary of the following: a man with no living relatives whatsoever (you're the only one that can help him); a man who lives or works far away (a nice excuse for why you can't meet in person); or a man with unusual speaking patterns or syntax (he's probably not a native English speaker and could actually be "catfishing" you from another country). These are all experiences I had within just a couple of months of being online.

Catfishing, by the way, is no longer just a reference to sitting in a boat casting out a line with sinkers and stink bait on the other end. It is now an action someone takes to lure you into a relationship via a fake profile. I've had quite a few people (who knows if this is limited to just men) attempt to catfish me, but I catch on pretty quickly. You have to be smarter than the average vertebrata on these dating websites. Just don't bite the hook with the stink bait on it!

After being approached by a man younger than my son who was brazen enough to offer me mind-blowing sex if I would just fund his lifestyle, I decided that a site dedicated to a more mature crowd was the second most logical choice for me. After all, this new site boasted of members who were fifty and over – you know those slightly graying, mature, established men that can contribute to the relationship. I pictured a single Sean Connery, Liam Neeson, or maybe even the edgier, Jon Bon Jovi clone just waiting to meet a woman who had her act together and was ready for a synergetic encounter!

For the third time, I changed my profile. Like Goldilocks, the first was too much; the second was too little; so maybe the third would be just right. Synergy seemed to be my new sought-after goal in a relationship; and without realizing it, I even paid homage to my yet-undiscovered kiddie-pool side:

> *Hello and thanks for checking out my profile! I'm just a genuine and faithful woman who is wanting to find that someone who is perfect for me. My family, faith, and values are important to me. If you smoke, if Jesus isn't your savior, or if you're just looking for a hook-up, I'm not your lady, but I wish you the best of luck in finding someone who is.*
>
> *I am looking for a real relationship that starts out as a friendship. In fact, I'm looking for that partner that will truly be my best friend. I'm just keeping it real here, but I prefer guys who have strong shoulders, metaphorically and literally. I have a variety of interests and a sense of adventure. I enjoy*

activities at home, but I also like to get out in the world and do things. I am looking for a guy who is intelligent, but that doesn't necessarily mean a college degree. Some of the smartest people I know just learned through life.

I didn't allow Alex to critique my new profile, so I wasn't sure how men would have interpreted my hopefully-improved attempt. Here was how I interpreted it: My values are important to me (not going to take my shirt off just because we've been on two dates); I can't handle smoke (not judging – too much just makes my throat sore); Jesus needs to be your savior (*spiritual* is open to too broad of an interpretation); I like shoulders (I'm a kiddie pool – muscles are important); I hope you're somewhat intelligent (I need a guy who can at least read. It would also be nice if he could spell and punctuate, but that's not an absolute requirement at this point).

On this new site, I actually made my first online dating friend, Beau; a retired New York state trooper. Beau and I had an uncommon bond: we were both the product of divorce after exactly thirty years of marriage. The difference was Beau had been the one to cheat. Through our long telephone conversations and his frank confessions, I was able to see the dissolution of my marriage from a perspective other than my own. I came to understand that while my ex's cheating was the death blow to our relationship, we both had faults and made choices that put us on a cold and dank path headed that direction. I intended on flying to New York to meet Beau in person, and he vowed to come run a marathon in Austin, so he could meet "Texas" as he nicknamed me.

7
Beneath Your Beautiful

In the midst of my online dating calamities, I took another divorced and sans kids vacation with Alex. We decided to head out for a week as platonic friends and explore Southern Colorado – a trip that coincided with my developing friendship with Beau. The trip was my idea. I couldn't wait to get back to Mesa Verde to hike Balcony House because I had only done it before with small children. I wanted to experience it without parental worries and distractions. So this was altogether new for me, and Alex had never been to this park that was once home to the Ancient Ones – the Anasazi cliff dwellers.

One morning during the trip, I received a text from Alex asking if I wanted to go workout. My immediate thought was "What part about vacation doesn't he understand?" But that thought was quickly followed by "Why the heck not?"

I was already dressed – just hadn't done hair or makeup and that could wait. So we searched out the Durango Recreation Center, and for six bucks each, we were admitted to the facilities, which boasted free weights, machines of all sorts, a jogging track, swimming pools, a hot tub and more.

I got on the elliptical and plugged in my music. My musical tastes are extremely eclectic, ranging from praise and worship to songs with a little "E" beside the title. That particular morning I chose my 70's playlist. I was still a little tired from hiking the cliff dwellings the day before, and I adopted a slow but steady pace for twenty minutes. I checked the room for Alex; he was on a stationary bike. I knew he came primarily to lift weights, so I guessed this was his warm-up activity.

I flashed back to the morning before when the absence of electricity and the clamor of voices outside my room woke me up. Our little motel community was hopping, and so I joined them. I could hear the river rushing below and trekked down to get a better look. I had never seen this part of the Animas so swollen and rapid. I talked to a few other tourists and really took in the location. That was heaven for me. And as Alex slept, I finished my morning routine and realized I had a little free time to grade some papers he had brought along, so I texted him that message. A minute later, he emerged from his room, sleepy-eyed, hair tousled, loose shorts, and no shirt. No shirt. So in the rec center at that moment, my mind connected to the work that built the shoulders and chest that occupied my shallow thoughts.

But my indulgence was interrupted by a text from New York. Typical for a Saturday morning, I grinned. Beau was just checking in to see how the trip was going – what the weather was like – what I was doing. I told him exercising, and he said he was midway through a thousand sit-ups. "Damn. That's hardcore," I replied and then began an arbitrary countdown, "475, 474, 473..." He reminded me he wanted to get out of New York a little the coming summer and meet up with me in Tennessee, the halfway point between us.

A few weeks before our Durango trip at a Ranger's game I had confided to Alex that I bought a plane ticket to fly to New York to meet Beau. Alex's mood changed to somber. I was never quite sure if it was because he was concerned for my safety, worried about my virtue, or perhaps a little jealous, but he actually asked me not to go to New York, and I agreed to get a refund on the ticket. If I knew anything, it was that Alex's friendship was important, and he didn't take my well-being lightly.

However, that morning in Durango on the elliptical reading Beau's licentious, flirty texts, I was just a little melancholy at the thought of giving up the ticket. I never did make the trip, but my happenstance with Beau was the first meaningful encounter I made online, and to this day, I'm fond of the upstate lawman-fisherman who introduced me to the lyrics of "Beneath Your Beautiful."

8
Cavemen and Spelunkers

So my dating journey continued to be a strange patchwork of traveling with Alex and going out with men I met online. Being in a car with Alex is an easy thing. Driving and riding for me are both pleasant. I'm visual and enjoy watching whatever is going on around me. *Scenic* has broad application – a worn billboard can be as captivating as a beautiful landscape. And I have a similar outlook on conversation – a mixture of casual, serious and even silence make up my playlist. I feel he's the same on both points, and that makes for traveling compatibility.

During the road trip we took out west, Alex and I decided to visit Carlsbad Caverns. I got first dibs at the radio and chose a playlist labeled "alternative" – songs with strong beats and weighty instrumentals, with voices that ranged from epic to airy. *Castle* by Halsey is representative of the group, and I forced Alex, whose taste is much more traditional than mine, to listen to it. And I sang out-of-tune, "I'm headed straight for the castle; they wanna make me their queen..." He raised an eyebrow at the thought of my monarch rule and switched off of the iPhone playlist to XM radio. I warned him when it was my turn to drive, I would be in charge of the music. Looking back, I drove very little.

Mostly we listened to hits from the '70s, '80s, and '90s. In what was unusual for me, I did not allow the music to influence my internal ruminations, with one distinct exception. Driving back from Roswell to our hotel in Carlsbad one night, Meatloaf's *Two Out of Three Ain't Bad* came on. It was one of my favorite songs growing up, and I always thought how sad for the protagonist in the ballad: "I want you, I need you, but there ain't no way I'm ever going to love you..." I had no point of reference for that as a teenager, but this trip, the song gained new meaning as I recalled Alex suggesting I find someone to date who would be cool with seeing me every other weekend and waiting for me to raise my daughter. He was not. He was looking for a lady whose kids were already grown as he had no interest in revisiting the role of stepfather and devoting his heart and resources to children he felt he could lose if the relationship with their mother turned sour. I think Alex and I were that kind of friends, "I want you, I need you, but there ain't no way I'm ever going to love you..." At least not romantically, we love each other dearly as friends.

Being with Alex was simply fun, and the drive to Carlsbad was indicative of that. I was seeing a part of Texas formerly foreign to me – dusty and worn, where the fracking underneath the ground seemed to have extracted as much from the life on top of it as it did below. Iron horses – or as Alex called them "grasshoppers" – bucked and neighed actively in barren fields and thriving neighborhoods alike, pumping the black oil that was the life-blood of these small towns.

We wandered off course several times to reminisce or to explore. We went to Seminole, where Alex had his first teaching job. Home of the black and gold Seminole Indians, Alex pointed out political correctness was not considered here. The facilities boasted an indoor practice field, and I was once again reminded of the value those pumping irons brought to the community.

We also took a detour through Gail, Texas and saw the Borden County Schools. I found interest in the brick pattern of the school that mimicked a butte towering in the distance. "Coyotes," Alex pointed out the mascot. I was impressed at his knowledge of mascots, and I lost count of the number we discussed on the trip. At one point he turned the trivia on me and asked if I could guess the Carlsbad mascot. I pride myself on being able to solve puzzles, so I thought I hit black gold with my answer, "the Carlsbad Spelunkers?" It seemed obvious, but alas, as I am prone to do, I overthought it and made it just a little too complicated. It is simply the Carlsbad Cavemen. Obviously, it was the football coach and not the English teacher that settled for that name!

9
Aliens and Authors

Alex and I arrived in Carlsbad a little earlier than planned and had an entire evening to fill and decided to catch a movie. With a little time to spare, we discovered a mall and stopped to explore. The mall was dismal, most of the spaces vacated and only a few unenthused souls milling about. A happenstance into an apparel store and conversation with Jasmine would change that.

Alex wanted a Caveman shirt – yes, the *actual* mascot of the town's school district, my brilliance be damned. The various Caveman illustrations and mottos were entertaining in and of themselves. Alex saw how he could quickly apply one of the shirt's slogans, "Whosoever holds this club, if he be worthy, shall possess the power of the Cavemen," to a baseball setting and made his choice. At the counter was Jasmine, the store manager, and we struck up a conversation with her about the town, who she was, who we were, that eventually led to the idea of driving to Roswell – much more imaginative than a movie!

As soon as we arrived in Roswell, we noticed gaudy green "aliens" hanging out at various establishments, helping managers capitalize on the lure of this otherwise un-noteworthy town. We circled the block behind the museum and looked for a place to park and an entrance into the mystery that is Roswell. The museum was closed, but Alex spied a sign on the building across the street that made him chuckle with curiosity, "Ancient of Days: Rocks, Fossils, Christian Supplies." Alex found it to be a peculiar juxtaposition, and I was drawn to the rock store on behalf of my collector father.

It turned out to be another great detour. I found two specimens indigenous to the area, Selenite and Aragonite, to purchase for my dad. Alex found the source of his amusement – a book by local author Guy Malone, *Come Sail Away with Me*. The premise is to reconcile the UFO phenomena and Christianity, to present aliens as demons. Alex had never heard this theory. I had heard it all my life.

The store manager told us during the day the author was often around to sign copies of the book, but he had left for the day. After only a little entreating, however, he also told us where he could be found – working the night shift at the Cattle Baron restaurant. It was a happy coincidence; we were famished! Guy the author became Guy our waiter. A pleasant and accommodating fella, he signed the book and patiently posed for a picture with the blonde stalker. Our dinner that night was amazing – green chili wontons, stuffed bacon-wrapped shrimp, and a burger made with brisket and ground sirloin.

After the meal, we were able to explore a little more as we found an open gift shop. A postcard caught my eye and made me snicker; it boasted, "What happens in Roswell, stays in Roswell," with the last part of the phrase struck out, so that the card read, "What happens in Roswell, DID NOT HAPPEN (U.S. Army Order 001.09.07.1947)."

I also found a book or two and a tiny green alien figurine to guard them on my bookshelf back home. I forced Alex to pose for a picture with me and a couple of aliens and asked the less-than-friendly store clerk to take it as part of my quest for documentation of my post-divorce life.

10
Hiding at the Bottom of a Cracker Jack Box

Alex and I spent that night in Carlsbad and got up early the next morning to be causal spelunkers ourselves. Initially, I had planned for us to hike the descent of the cave to the underground lobby where tours begin, but we didn't allow the hour required, so we took the elevator. As we were waiting to get on the one-stop cable box, the liftman of old gave instructions and a description of the trip down – the 750-foot trip down. I quickly did some math in my head; and at approximately ten feet per story, that is roughly seventy-five stories underground. As we stepped into the steel box, I tried to wrap my head around just how far of a drop that was, how fast the elevator would likely move, and how long I would be on it; my palms started to sweat. I got a glimpse of the back side of the elevator. There is a wall that hosts a rectangular window down the center. Fantastic, a view?! My slight fear of elevators increased as did the sweat in my tightened fists. I reached and grabbed Alex's hand and guided his fingers to touch my palms as a silent signal of how nervous I was.

The elevator doors opened into a large expanse. I've explored many caves, but I instantly knew this was something different. The foyer of the cave alone is a huge commercially-developed room with a dining area and kiosks for gifts, drinks, and food.

I was in a discordant state as my senses recovered from the sudden change in altitude and temperature and adjusted to dim artificial light while my mind was assaulted by the concurrence of commercial and natural.

We had a little time before our guided tour, so we ventured slightly on a self-guided path. Quickly, I left behind the mercantile and discovered geological novelty and splendor unlike anything I had ever seen. The mammoth cave is a wonder for its size alone, one massive chamber emptying into another and a seemingly endless bounty of nooks, crannies, and undeveloped trails; but it is also decorated with countless magnificent cave formations. Stalactites, stalagmites, soda straws, popcorn, pearls, draperies, flowstone, and more adorn the chambers and create a world of enchantment that invited my imagination to see other worlds.

On the guided tour, Alex commented about creativity – we both believe that it is a process that can be taught and learned. It seemed he was still in a Roswell-state-of-mind as he suggested plots and settings related to outer space and made a case for science fiction. I saw it too – science fiction, fairytales, the supernatural. It was like watching clouds take shape and then morph into something different before your eyes – only the "clouds" were innumerable fixed formations, and the liquid illusion was created as your eyes danced about the landscape.

We joined the guided tour and hiked an hour and a half of trails displaying water-formed wonders that culminate in the King's Palace, an eight-story descent into the deepest developed part of the cave. With the guide, we got to experience cave darkness – and after a few of us got our phones reigned in (or turned off), we experienced a total absence of light.

The moment brought to mind a common syllogism: *Darkness does not exist; it is the absence of light. Cold does not exist either; it is the absence of heat. Evil does not exist per se; it is the absence of God.* I grimly pondered being cast into outer darkness, and it followed that weeping and gnashing of teeth would be the byproduct of eternal sense deprivation and eventual insanity. Cave darkness is intense.

In my morbid ruminations, The *Bottomless Pit* was an attraction of the cave that piqued my curiosity. After we left the group, we turned left to head to the unguided portion of the tour where we saw *Rock of Ages*, *Mirror Lake*, and the sought-after destination. Personally, I enjoyed the unguided portion of the cave just a little more. Placards along the way provided almost as much information as our former guide, who seemed only to have memorized what was on the cue cards and not to know much else. Each point of interest embodied a novel set of formations that ranged from massive to delicate, flowing to jagged, gypsum to calcite; so that I felt like I was privileged to fresh tableaux each twist of the pathway.

Bottomless Pit did not disappoint. Years ago, explorers discovered that what gave the impression of bottomless – we were staring into a large, black hole that seemed without limits – actually had a floor 140 feet below the opening. The expanse from the ceiling above the hole to the floor beneath the opening is 370 feet. Standing at 140 feet, I felt an overwhelming sense of exposure and almost got dizzy looking up at *Liberty Dome*. Alex cautiously sidled up to the railing beside me and embraced his fear of heights, allowing the sensation to wash over him and send an ominous shudder to his core. Or at least that's what I sensed happened.

After hours of trapesing around the cave, we rested and divvied a sandwich back in the underground lobby. He shared descriptions of how the lobby looked years ago and what was different now. As we shared a sandwich, I looked at Alex in the belly of the cave, recalled the song, and hummed silently, "There ain't no Coup de Ville hiding at the bottom of a Cracker Jack box." Maybe that line would be my theme if it came to looking for something more in my friendship with Alex. Up to this point, it also seemed to be the case for my online dating escapades.

11
Stingrays and Butterflies

My grown son did his best to put his two cents in when it came to my dating life. He told me I might want to reconsider taking my shirt off on the third date if I really hoped to have much luck, and he was almost angry that I couldn't make it work with a guy who had a seven-hundred-acre ranch. Jake embodies the hunter-fisherman stereotype. In fact, if his wife had not adamantly vetoed it, he considered naming his firstborn Hunter Fisher.

Jake also gave me all sorts of tips on how to be a better dater. Buy a bass boat, learn to cook, and be willing to get naked – were just a few. In his quest to turn me into a woman more palatable to men, he taught me how to bow fish. Actually, it was really fun going out to the river near my house and sneaking up on the dam at night. We used red light to illuminate the small carp and gar that swam close enough to the surface to make easy targets. In spite of Jake's expert instruction, I only came close to the targets and never actually hit one.

He decided I needed a bigger target and eventually chartered a boat one night when we were staying in Gulf Shores, Alabama. Along with my daughter-in-law, Hali, and her dad, we went on a stingray hunt with a guide. It was exhilarating.

I always thought of myself as a lover of nature and never realized I would be enthralled by the hunt and not at all disturbed by the harpooning of an innocent and magnificent creature. I held my trophies up proudly on the deck, blood dripping on my legs and white boat shoes, as I grinned for the camera. I got two.

Now let me explain quickly, you don't actually kill the stingray. I'm not saying the process is painless for the poor cartilaginous fish, but it is not deadly. The arrows are made in such a way that they have a release barb and slide out with little damage. As long as you don't hit the stingray in the direct center of its body, it swims away after the photo op.

When I met Shawn online, there seemed to be potential. He believed in God, ran cattle on a large farm, knew how to work on trucks, and drank his coffee black. Was this a manly man or what? (Seriously, I could picture the two of us on the deck of a boat, my hand resting lightly on his shoulder as he drew back on a monster ray.) We messaged back and forth for quite a long time before we actually talked on the phone, and I was excited at the prospect of meeting Shawn. He seemed to have viable employment, strong family ties, and good morals – all things I had stopped taking for granted when it came to meeting men online.

I will never forget the exact moment I received his first call. I was sitting with my legs crossed in the middle of my bed going through some notes for a presentation I had to make the next morning. When my cell buzzed, butterflies took flight on cue. I tried to calm my nerves, quell my anticipation, and steady my voice before I finally answered and said, "Hello." And in less than a few seconds, the butterflies dropped dead of disappointment. The caller had only said, "Hi, Keri. This is Shawn," but he had said it in a voice that was nothing but soprano. I lowered my head in shame. I was the shallowest of shallow, but I could not imagine taking a man bow fishing with me who would express, "I nailed one," with the high-pitched voice of a teenaged girl.

12
Epiphany in Margaritaville

I suppose one way to lure women on a dating site is to have a claim to fame. Miguel, for instance, told me that Santana, of *Black Magic Woman* fame, was his cousin. Since they both shared a surname and love for music, I didn't doubt it was the truth. I am actually a huge fan of Santana and must admit it did increase my interest in Miguel. However, we never actually went on a date, so to my disappointment, I didn't get to meet the quintessential guitarist either.

I did, however, get to meet David #2. While David and I actually met online, we knew a lot of the same people in my hometown, so we agreed that if it worked out, we would come up with a better story than meeting online.

I've always been amazed by people who were in a grocery store or something, and they bump into a total stranger, and blah, blah, blah…they're married. I mean, how does that even happen? I go to the grocery store on at least a weekly basis. In all those trips, I am pretty sure I have never seen a single eligible man shopping there; let alone one I could "accidentally" bump my cart into for the sole purpose of engaging in a meaningful conversation that leads to him asking me out; yet, this seems to happen in movies quite frequently and, therefore, must have some modicum of reasonability.

I have put on my best Friday night outfit and dolled up my face with smoky eyes and all just to saunter into the grocery store on a Monday afternoon and peruse with my cart up and down each aisle looking for a poor bachelor to ambush. Somehow, however, they keep eluding me. If David #2 and I hit it off, I devised a plan to tell everyone that I saw him in the produce section and explained to him how to pick out a cantaloupe, and he was so impressed with my knowledge of melons and concern for his palette that he asked me back to his place, and the rest is history.

In reality, on our first date, I pulled up to the appointed meeting place (which actually was the local grocery store parking lot), arriving just a couple of minutes late. The white Toyota Tundra was waiting, so I parked quickly, driver's door to driver's door with enough empty space to provide a gap to meet in the middle. He stepped out, and I drew in a quick breath. From his pics, I thought he was a nice-looking man; from his profile, tall; but I wasn't prepared for the strikingly handsome statuesque man who stepped out of the truck and towered over me.

I smiled, trying to gauge his reaction to the 5'4" blonde donned in a black blouse and comfortable jeans and hidden behind her favorite pair of sunglasses. The look on his face was reassuring. We exchanged a quick introduction and a hug before he escorted me to the passenger side of the vehicle. We had a forty-five-minute drive to the restaurant, so we engaged in conversation, mostly about how awkward first dates were.

We actually went to a steakhouse instead of a Mexican food restaurant. I bet you were beginning to wonder if Texas even has steakhouses. Of course, we do! Texas boasts more cattle than any other state in the U.S., and Texans pride themselves on consuming red meat, the redder the better. In fact, we prefer our steaks to moo just a little.

It was crowded, but we were lucky to find a table in the bar area. The manager came over and asked what we'd like to drink. I hesitated for a second, wanting to order a piña colada, but not remembering if David drank or not. The urge for the creamy concoction won out, and he followed by ordering a Miller Lite. And the conversation continued: private school in Mississippi, his football career, his brother playing for the Crimson Tide, his son; my start in education, my grandson, the various places in Texas I've lived.

For dinner, I ordered my Saltgrass standby, steak with a side of stuffed barbequed shrimp en brochette, and he decided to give the entrée a try also. We discussed those topics people our age must brooch: prior marriages and divorces, what went wrong, who was at fault, what was the fallout. My story is already stale as far as I'm concerned, so I only hit the highlights: my ex's midlife crisis, lost job, new car, and new girlfriend.

He described briefly the demise of his second marriage, her affair. I noticed a tremor in his hand, and he explained it was hereditary. I found the imperfection strangely reassuring; in spite of being devilishly handsome, he was just a normal guy.

The manager checked on us for the third time, and David said, "I think he has a crush on you." I suggested maybe he was just eavesdropping on our juicy first-date tête-à-tête. We laughed. The conversation was easy and flowing. We enjoyed a delicious meal, and he commented I have good taste. He picked up the check, and we decided to go play pool, coincidentally, at the same establishment where I had played ping pong with David #1. The place was not crowded, nor was it smoke-filled.

Playing pool provided the opportunity to further observe details. My date was a good player who understood where to leave the cue ball for the next shot. He called each pocket. He rarely missed. I knew I would not beat this guy, so I decided to learn from him. And by the end of the night, I shot the best pool of my life. Albeit I only won two of the eight games, both because he scratched on the final shot, and I was pretty sure, intentionally. I mentally compared the two men who share the same first name – the one who beat me forcefully and the one who won humbly. David #2 was definitely winning the dating game.

At one point he seemed to be taking extra time lining up the shot when he stopped and looked up at me. He said, "Keri, I just have to say I can't imagine any man letting such a beautiful woman go." I blushed and managed, "Thank you." I meant it; I was truly grateful for the compliment even if I was sure it was exaggerated. The ending of a marriage and the uncertainty of online dating can take its toll on a girl's ego. It was comforting to know David found me attractive.

A band began to hammer out classic rock from the '70s and '80s. I didn't try to contain the rhythm that oozed out as my hips picked up the beat and small undulations surfaced in my shoulders – subtle movements that confirmed the comfort and pleasure of the situation. And maybe he noticed or maybe it was because the volume of the band forced the proximity to hear the conversation, but he began to stand closer and put his arm around me. Time passed quickly, and it was late too soon. Very late.

    I can't ever remember a drive home being as short. We arrived at my car, and I hugged David and told him I had a really good time and enjoyed his company. It was honest. When we parted, I received a text, "I enjoyed your company as well! You're a very pretty and a classy lady, Keri. We'll have to do it again soon if you're willing." I smiled, correct punctuation for a noun of direct address and proper use of a homophone – maybe this was going to be something after all. So I replied, "Sure! Just let me know." But as I walked into my bedroom and saw a picture of Alex and me in Carlsbad, I felt a wave of regret. Getting close to David – dating him even – meant my lifestyle might have to change.

    I thought about how important my independence had become, and how I loved running the roads with Alex; I revisited the date with David and found myself making an illogical comparison. David was taller, played pool a little better, expressed his attraction freer – winked and smiled and touched. I thought about how he lived in the area, worked in the area, didn't mind raising another child; but somehow I preferred hanging out with my friends. Suddenly, when it comes to lack of success in online dating, I have an epiphany: I'm at the last stanza of a Jimmy Buffet song, "And I know it's my own damn fault."

    And, sure enough, it was my fault, and David #2 sensed I had some commitment issues – or maybe he just found someone he liked better – and after three dates, he broke it off. The quintessential gentleman, he made a very polite exit, and I wished him the best. In hindsight, I wished I wouldn't have been so introspective and, instead, invested a little more. Too much overthinking, and I let a good one get away. However, my life made an unexpected turn. I still sensed God wanted me to be still, and it was all moot point anyway.

Part 2: Letters from Leavenworth

13
Same Kind of Weird

I had dismissed Tammy numerous times when in the midst of all my failed attempts at dating she would say, "My brother would be perfect for you. You guys are so much alike." If I'm completely honest, she would say, "You guys are the same kind of weird." I knew of Tammy's brother. He was a former Army Ranger with an outstanding, highly decorated career. Every time I visited her house, one of the first things I would see when I walked into her foyer was a picture of her and one of her sisters with him when they had visited him in Germany – right before the trial. John was serving his seventh year of a forty-year sentence in Leavenworth for military crimes, convicted of killing four Iraqi insurgents. While I was familiar with the case and completely believed John was innocent, I was not the type of woman who had anything to do with a man in prison. Or so I thought.

About two years after my divorce, Tammy came into the office one day and was noticeably less chipper than she was every other day of the year. Tammy, as you recall, is the eternal optimist, and barring something tragic, she's never in a bad mood or not smiling. But that day she was obviously sad, so I inquired as to what was wrong, and she shared with me that her family had received the results of her brother's sentence commutation hearing. His sentence had been reduced from forty years to twenty-five, which was good, but the family thought that made him eligible for immediate parole and that he might be released that year. They had just learned he wouldn't be eligible until August the following year. It meant at least another thirteen months in prison.

Other than the conviction, John had an exemplary military career, and he had demonstrated excellent behavior in prison. He was the highest ranking non-commissioned officer to be imprisoned at Leavenworth, and although military prisoners lose their rank, the other inmates respected him. Highly disciplined and pragmatic, he made it clear to his default roommates his new "home" would be a place where they would live by the same code he'd always insisted on in his military unit. In the time he had already served, assaults and fights within his prison unit became nearly non-existent.

Tammy was really sad, and I had no idea how to make her feel better, but for the first time, I felt compelled to write her brother, and that was how I responded to the situation:

Dear John,

> *I know we've never met in person, but this is Keri, and I'm a good friend of your sister Tammy. I've been acquainted with Tammy for a while, but I didn't really know Tammy well until I came to work here and inherited her as my secretary. Secretary, by the way, is the wrong word. She's the brains of the operation, my right-hand woman, the light in the room – much better descriptions! Tammy and the*

others here in my office have become my family and make coming to work a joy.

I'm not sure why I'm writing this letter, except that today Tammy's heart was broken when she learned you would not be released. She tried to smile through the tears and look on the bright side and trust God's plan, but I can see she's deeply hurting. As family, we all hurt when one does, and we pull out all of the stops to try to make it better. Of course, there are some things we just can't fix. It's killing me that I can't really do something to make this better for Tammy – and for you and her family by extension.

Anyway, I just had the overwhelming desire to share with you stories about your sister. She's so funny and beautiful and intelligent. I've had the good fortune to spend lots of time with her over the past four and a half years – time you've been robbed of – so I thought if you didn't mind, I'd share a little of my perspective of your sister with you a letter at a time. So there's the grocery store story...

A few years back, Tammy ran into the local grocery store to buy some groceries. When she got inside, she heard a man yell loudly across the store, "Miss Tammy, Miss Tammy..." Now this man is since deceased, and I'm pretty sure Tammy had nothing to do with it, but he finished that sentence with, "Your legs sure are getting fat!" You can imagine that Tammy was completely mortified – to the point she immediately left the store without purchasing a single item. I tell you this because Tammy is nothing but drop-dead gorgeous – but she's always complaining about her legs or ankles. That's just the way women work – we pick one flaw and *make a tall-tale out of it. But to her credit, Tammy is the one who told me that story and laughs with me every time it gets retold. That's one of the many things I love about your sister. She doesn't take herself too seriously and can eventually laugh at just about any situation.*

John, I am so sorry to learn the parole board's decision was only to reduce your sentence and not to completely rectify this situation. I know your sister misses you and misses the opportunity for "whole" family gatherings and the such. I know she relishes a life for you beyond those prison walls. But I also know she's faithful and an optimist, and she's strong. I can only imagine you must be all these things as well.

I hope I didn't take too great a liberty in writing this letter, but by knowing and loving Tammy and being close to her, I feel just a little bit close to you, too.

Keri

I didn't know if John would write me back – I didn't even expect him to. It was simply a way of doing something for Tammy when there was really nothing I could do that would matter. To my surprise, a week or so later, I received a letter back from John:

Dear Keri,

Thank you for writing your letter. I do appreciate you taking the time out of your busy schedule and writing. I hope this letter finds you doing great. Tammy mentioned you to me about a year ago during a visit, and she and Ricky [Tammy's husband] spoke very highly of you. You are quite accomplished. As a matter of fact, I believe I've seen you in the local newspaper, so you're actually quite famous! I mean not my kind of famous; but trust me, you don't want my kind of famous. Lol!

As for the Parole Board, although it obviously did not go quite the way I wanted it, I honestly didn't expect very much. After twenty years of being in the military and another seven years in here, I've learned not to get my hopes up. My family is my greatest concern because although I'm used to not getting my hopes up, my family hasn't quite mastered it yet. I am thankful Tammy has someone like you for support. Fortunately, our family has all been raised to deal with anything life throws at us, so I feel we are all pretty optimistic. Like Pop says, "A hundred years from now, none of this will even matter!"

With any luck, I hope to be out by next August. Until then, I will just keep working on my MBA. After I get out, I'll start my business while simultaneously working on my Masters in Social Work. I am really looking forward to doing that and building my house.

I loved your story about Tammy! She has mentioned several similar stories, and they're all funny. You may not have noticed this, but our family is never short of stories! Lol! All four of my sisters came up to visit me a few years ago. We (they, of course) were so rowdy, I thought we might all get kicked out of visitation, but believe it or not, I've been kicked out of a lot better places than this. Actually, we discussed this and hoped they would just say, "Okay, that's it; take him with you and just leave. We have to get some peace and quiet around here." It didn't work. Maybe next time.

By no means did you take great liberty in writing to me. I enjoyed your letter and hope to hear from you again. As Tammy is a testament to, I don't know if our family has ever really met any strangers. Well, none stranger than me anyway.

I'll keep it short for now because I don't want to bore you too much. You know, there is just not a lot that changes around here. I may need a class on how to act around decent folks again before I get out of here. So if you have any pointers, feel free to let me know. You and the girls in the office could maybe come up with a "Do" and "Don't" list of things for me to study. What do you think? There are some advantages I have realized from being here. For example, if you've never had a toilet just one foot away from the end of your bed, well, you just don't know what you're missing! Why didn't I ever think of that before???? It may have been because I spent too much time living in the woods or the desert that I just didn't know what I was missing. Hmmm...something to think about.

Take care, and again, thank you for writing. I really did enjoy your letter.

John

I was not only surprised by the quick reply, but I had no idea how personable John was. I instantly liked him and decided to tell him as much when I wrote him back:

Dear John,

I'm so glad you replied! From your letter, you are instantly likable! I love your easy mannerisms, that you don't take yourself too seriously, and that you have a positive outlook. Those are all good traits in my opinion, and all traits you share with Tammy. We will pray next August has a different outcome!
I have been on vacation and out of the office for a week so far. While I don't miss the work, I miss the people. I can't wait to discuss with the girls your dilemma of adjusting to life on the outside. I'm sure we can come up with some do's and don'ts for you, but one jumps out at me immediately: Don't stand up in the middle of the night and pee beside your bed! Although you're used to the convenience on the inside, you will have to change your nighttime routine once you're out here. I can't think of a single person with a bedside toilet in their house as a fixture! There's the funky odor problem, the flushing that wakes up the other person in the bed (assuming there's another person in the bed), and the obvious aesthetic nuisance! You will just have to learn to bite the bullet like the rest of us and take the extra twenty steps to the bathroom.
My story about Tammy today is actually a little more about Ricky. You know they are dog lovers, and Ricky especially loves his Whippet. Well, Tammy and Ricky were in Home Depot not too long ago, and for a reason I cannot remember, Ricky threatened to "sick his Whippet" on some guy who apparently did not know that a Whippet is a dog breed. He reacted as if Ricky was making some weird move on him, but Ricky didn't get it. Tammy did –

and was laughing so hard she started choking. Ricky is such a funny guy that I can totally picture this whole scene – Ricky trying to be menacing and imagining his faithful pup taking up his cause; this confused man trying to find a point of reference for "whip it" and all that comes to mind is the crazy Devo song, "Whip it. Whip it good," or worse, some "50 Shades of Grey" paraphernalia and Ricky in the role of the dominant. Ha!

Speaking of Tammy and Ricky, they have been a sort of yardstick for me. I guess Tammy told you I got a divorce after thirty years of marriage. It's an ugly story, but it's been two years, and I have gandered new perspective and, I hope, a little wisdom in the process. Tammy and Ricky make me optimistic about second chances – they seem to be best friends and genuinely like hanging out together. They each survived a previous marriage to find one another. While I'm not a proponent of divorce, things happen, and I hope to someday find something similar to what they have.

Well, as you can see, I love to write – and I don't think I've ever met a stranger either. If you want to continue to be pen pals, I would really enjoy that. I believe that in life what matters are the people you come across, the interactions you have with them, and the relationships you build.

Take care, John, and thanks for writing me back!

Keri

14
A Prison Pen Pal

And thus, our pen-pal relationship had begun. Life continued on as normal for both of us with the exception that every few days, we would each receive a letter in the mail and write one in return. John shared with me funny stories that related to his time in the military or in prison, family anecdotes, and personal aspirations. I shared with him my background, my exploits, and my hopes and dreams as well. I can't say when we shifted from strangers to friends, but it didn't seem to take long:

Dear Keri,

Of course, I replied. What kind of inmate do you take me for??? Actually, I'm a horrible correspondent. I hope one of these days I'll improve exponentially, but I'm not holding my breath for me to change anytime soon. Besides, who wouldn't want to write you back? You are pretty funny you know? A lot of the time I just get so absorbed in my coursework I lose track of everything else I should be accomplishing. Who would have guessed you can stay so busy in prison? See, we don't all just lift weights!

Okay, you mentioned you went on vacation, but you didn't mention where you went. You do understand I live vicariously through all of you on the outside? Did you do anything exciting: swim with the dolphins, skydive, travel to another country, kiss the Blarney Stone, etc.? By the way, what is it exactly that you do enjoy? Lay it on me, sister. Give me all the nitty-gritty.

Duly noted about the toilet protocol; you'll have to forgive us knuckle-dragging Neanderthals. After spending twenty years in the infantry and another almost eight years in the hoosegow, I'm sure you can understand that I may need to brush up on my etiquette. Fortunately, I feel confident I can be re-indoctrinated into civil society. Fingers crossed.

I did love the story you told me about Ricky in Home Depot. And despite what you might have been led to believe by Tammy, the fact you've read "50 Shades of Grey" was not the only thing I took away from that story...

I do enjoy receiving your letters, and I would like to continue to be pen pals. I agree completely with you about what matters in life are the people you come across, the interactions you have with them, and the relationships you build. Additionally, I feel life is made up of a few defining moments and how you react in the face of those adversities is what defines you. You can never let others or your environments define your life. You are obviously an incredibly special person, and remember, you're the one who came out ahead in the divorce.

Okay, I apologize for getting so philosophical. I didn't mean to get carried away. So on a lighter note, have you ever been to any other countries? I love to travel, and as you can imagine, being in the military provided me with numerous opportunities. I think at last count I have been to somewhere between twenty-five to thirty countries. But I still have several places I would like to travel. The country I *most enjoyed living in would have to be Germany, but the most beautiful city I have been to would be Paris. I really did love the architecture. I have numerous locations on my bucket list I'd still like to visit. I want to walk and ride a motorcycle along portions of the Great Wall of China and backpack through Cambodia, Laos, Vietnam, and Thailand. I also want to go to Scotland, Ireland, and England. I had opportunities to go there, but I let them slip by. I love submersing myself in other cultures...*

Although John didn't reference his traveling aspirations as a "bucket list," I was hooked. He seemed to have a sense of adventure that superseded my own. I let him know, however, he was much more badass than I would ever be. I had no illusions that I could successfully keep up on a backpacking trip in a jungle, which as I imagined, would be teeming with all sorts of dangers and inconveniences.

At a future point, he would invite me to go backpacking with him (upon his release, of course), and I responded that I didn't have the stamina for it and would inevitably fall behind. His response to that was, "If you fell behind, I'd pick you up and carry you." It might have been an exaggeration, but it seemed indicative of the man I was getting to know and the kind of man I wanted in my life. His whole life and career had been about serving his country and making sure no one was ever left behind – of blindly storming into danger, more concerned about the safety of those he led than his own.

Dear John,

First, how fun is this that I'm writing "Dear John" letters?! Ha!
I enjoyed every line you wrote in your last letter – I literally laughed to the point of tears. You are incredibly witty. I'm not even sure where to begin, so I'll just dive in.
I absolutely LOVE to travel, but I've only been overseas once to London with my ex. However, I've traveled the continental US quite a bit. Recently, I made a trip with my kids to the beach. I have a twenty-eight-year-old son who is married and has a precocious two-and-a-half- year old. My daughter is eleven. The five of us traveled by car to Gulf Shores, Alabama and Perdido Key, Florida. You haven't lived until you've ridden in the backseat with an "independent" toddler for nine hours!
Jase calls me Gigi, and he has my heart wrapped around his proverbial little finger; he is equally adorable and toot – you never know who will show up to the party. His latest test of my patience is to tell me, "Gigi, don't you say those words to me!" (I've adopted this as my own catchphrase when I don't like someone's message as well.) We did what we could do with the little ones – a dolphin cruise, swimming in the ocean, fishing on a large pier, visiting an alligator farm, etc. My daughter caught a sucker fish – the kind that hitches a ride on a shark – and she let it "attach" to her hand. It was pretty cool. We were able to see sharks from the pier, as well as dolphins, jellyfish, and stingrays. I waded out into the ocean one night when there was a full moon – sharks be damned – it was so cool!

Okay, this might be a good time to tell you just a little more about me. My life is a bit of a dichotomy. (Now that you've used "loquacious," I feel compelled to show you I learned something in school as well!) I have strong faith, and I'm a Christian who loves God completely, but I have a spicy side – probably to God's dismay. (He's not done with me yet!) That translates to a salty vocabulary at times and an eclectic taste in music and literature – not that I'm calling "50 Shades" literature by any means, but you did deduce correctly that I had read it. My life motto used to be, "You never know what is enough until you know what is more than enough." Age, and I'm a little older than you, has tempered me a little, but I'm still inclined to test the limits.

The second week of my vacation I spent in New Mexico and West Texas with a good friend – male, platonic. You have to know I am enamored with nature. I still get excited by a rainbow! For me, creation is about the creator, and I can't get enough of it. So you can imagine how ecstatic I was on this last trip when God blessed me by getting to see the rings of Saturn...

Of course, I went on to share my story about seeing the rings of Saturn and told him I believed in messages from God. And I shared other things from my bucket list, even relating some of the things I had gotten to check off. Last year for my birthday, Alex and I had taken Salsa dancing lessons, which of course was on the list. As far as dancing went, I still wanted to Tango in public, be part of a flash mob, and somehow get to play around on aerial silks.

His response to my letter was humorous, starting out with, "Isn't dichotomy just another word for schizophrenic?" He then assured me we could be friends even if I was a little crazy. He noticed my children's ages were disparate and asked if that was planned or just a happy surprise. He mentioned we both had big life changes at forty – I had a baby, and he went to prison. He was pretty sure I had fared better. As far as our slight age gap, he mentioned he was certain he looked older than me as infantry years are hard years. What I liked most about him was his sense of adventure and wonder for nature, which was so similar to mine:

> ... *One of the few good things about the Middle East is that you can see the stars from horizon to horizon in a 360° panorama. It's awesome to witness. When my family moved to Alaska, we drove up there from Texas. On the side of the road somewhere in Canada, the trailer we were pulling broke down. It wasn't all bad. It was colder than a witch's tit, but we did get to see the Aurora Borealis...*

I made a mental note. This had been on my bucket list since its inception. He continued:

> ...*I think you would like the jungle. I've spent a little bit of time in the jungles in Panama and Honduras. In Honduras, we ran a few missions, but in Panama, I was there for jungle operations training. I loved it there. I would have gotten stationed there if I could. It can get spooky, but it's how you know you're alive. You know, if it doesn't kill you...lol!*

> *What you have to be careful of is getting addicted to adrenaline rushes. It's easy to find yourself chasing that rush. You want to hear something funny? The last time my mama visited she asked if I thought maybe it was a good thing I went to prison. She said she didn't mean it in a bad way, but she was always afraid I would have gone right back to combat as a contractor after I retired, which was exactly what I had planned. She was afraid I would never leave that life. So see, maybe you're right about messages.*
>
> *Now although I think I've gotten rid of that adrenaline addiction, there are still some things I'll do. I went snowboarding for the first time at forty, and I still plan on doing that again. Have you ever been? It's fun. I won't say I'm very good, but it's kind of like sex. You don't have to be good at it to enjoy it. Lol! Sorry!*
>
> *...I like your creative list, too. I even thought about learning to Salsa, but the Tango sounds cool as well. Hopefully, I wouldn't look like a baboon with two club feet. Although, when I lived in Korea, some of my Korean friends called me "bi gon won sincee," which means red monkey. Surely that was because the hair on my arms had a red tint from the sun. At least that's what I tell myself.*

His letters were transparent enough that I felt like I gained great insight into his personality. I think he survived his situation by trying to add humor whenever possible:

> *...Here at the barber shop, when I was an instructor, one of the guys asked me what kind of jobs I had worked before I joined the Army. So I named off*

several jobs, and then he asked what was the worst job I had ever had. Now there are over twenty-four people in here practicing straight razor shaves when I started telling them about working at the LaGrange Chicken Ranch in Texas. I told them there were about a hundred employees that worked there. About twenty-five worked on the regular side and about seventy-five of us worked on the boneless side. This was the hardest part of the work because since the chickens don't have any bones and are just lying in the yard, we have to go by each one and pick their heads up and feed and water them. I told him how exhausting it was to have to do every hour. One of the guys that grew up in the city said, "Yo! You for real? Hell, I don't want that job." Everybody about exploded. I don't know how somebody didn't get cut, but I'm sure if they would have, I would have gotten blamed.

    Back in the office, I read this part of his letter to Darla, who responded, "Are there really boneless chickens?" Have I mentioned Darla is a transplant from California? No self-respecting country girl would have ever asked that question.
    A few weeks later, John sent me a travel magazine in the mail. He had gone through the magazine and highlighted a few things and made some notes. He was certainly appealing to my wanderlust. I replied to his sending the magazine:

John,

    I came home at lunch today and checked my mail. I was pleasantly surprised to get a letter from you and the travel magazine. You certainly earned some bonus points by taking the time to send me "Islands," but more importantly, by knowing exactly what parts I would find intriguing!

The manatee swim party and stargazing affair are a close tie for my top spot! I love animals and can only imagine the novelty and serenity I'd experience being up close and personal with those benign beasts. And you already know how I feel about the stars! My bucket list is growing and adding some specificity – I now actually want to take the expedition up Mauna Kea and snorkel in the Crystal River. Be careful, though, since you brought these things to my attention, I may just decide you need to accompany me on these exploits!

The waterfalls featured in the pictures were beautiful – also wonders of this natural world I'm drawn too. I also don't mind mixing it up a little. A "Haunted History Bermuda Tour" might just be a zany way to top off an evening and be adventurous on all accounts.

I was not only adding to my bucket list, but I began to see him as the ideal traveling companion. We talked about everything; I wanted to know what it was like to grow up as a preacher's kid and about his past relationships. There didn't seem to be any boundaries to what I could inquire, so I even asked how he responded to people who asked why he was in prison. He told me he stole the line from *Ronin*, "I hurt someone's feelings once."

As far as being a preacher's kid, he told me he got his fair share of sermons but religion was never forced down this throat. From his stories about his childhood antics, I could tell he gave his parents more than one occasion to need a stiff drink. That must have been hard on a Baptist preacher and his wife! Once he asked me what was my favorite perfume, and with his situation in mind, I responded:

I like two – one very cheap and one moderately expensive – although I only wear perfume lightly and not every day. The more expensive one is Miracle by Lancôme. It's a modern, oriental fragrance with a fruity opening (litchi); slightly spiced flowery heart (magnolia, jasmine, ginger, and pepper); and powdery base of musk and amber. In other words, it's soft and floral.

The inexpensive fragrance I like is Tabu by Dana. They couldn't be more different. Miracle was created in 2000; Tabu in 1932. Tabu is a blend of bergamot, coriander, neroli, orange, and spices; a heart of clove bud oil, clover, jasmine, narcissus, oriental rose, and ylang-ylang; and a base of amber, benzoin, cedar, civet, moss, musk, patchouli, sandalwood, and vetiver. In short, it's spicy and musky. It's a scent you either love or hate. I went to dinner many years ago with a friend and mentor who asked me what perfume I was wearing, and I said "Tabu." He replied it was his all-time favorite fragrance. My son absolutely hates it. The man who created it, Jean Carles, is the same man who created Christian Dior's Miss Dior. He's quite renowned for his expertise in the field.

I was concerned about the sensory deprivation of being imprisoned; the drab colors – off-white, tans, or grays; limited windows, extremely narrow and double pained with thick bullet-proof glass that marred the view; a place that smelled of institutional food and generic cleaning supplies. I imagined there was little aesthetically pleasing to the eyes or the nose, and I wanted John to have a real sense of the fragrances through my description.

Although nothing in life is certain, I never doubted he would be released when August rolled around, and I caught myself time after time in the mindset that his incarceration wouldn't be much longer. In letter after letter, we increasingly revealed more and more about ourselves. But not everything was a match. He had a great deal of concern about the dissolution of my thirty-year marriage and was unhappy that I still allowed my ex to have so much influence, especially when it came to my daughter. As a trained soldier and admitted prepper, he found my serendipitous approach to life and safety a little unnerving. He also admitted to me his faith wasn't where mine was:

> ... I grew up in a strong Christian family, and it has given me a strong moral base, but I'm not particularly religious. I've witnessed some pretty horrific things in war and lost numerous friends in combat that have raised questions for me. Also, being sent to prison for something I didn't do didn't improve my situation. After I'm released, I'll go to church, but that's more out of respect for my folks. I actually support religion if it keeps people from acting like lunatics. I'm not sure if this will make sense to you...

It made perfect sense. Although he still adhered

to the values his parents had instilled, he now questioned God, especially God's role in a world full of inequities and atrocities. I dismissed the fact we weren't on the same page because I believed one day when the imprisonment was behind him, he would return to his roots. He also included this:

> *By the way, what's your take on tattoos? In case you have not been informed, I have one or two...or six. Of course, these don't count the Care Bear or My Little Pony I have on each ass cheek, but I don't include those because you usually don't see those in public. Usually. And, no, I didn't get those in prison! Why does everyone always ask me that?*

Forever the clown! I did start to wonder what my family would think if they knew not only was I corresponding with an inmate – a convicted quadruple murderer at that – his arms and chest were covered in tattoos to boot. I think it was safe to assume I would no longer be viewed as Miss Good Bar, a nickname my brothers had given me growing up because I was always the goody-two-shoes of the family. And it was more than corresponding. I liked this guy. To mixed reception, I let my parents, kids, and even Alex, in on my latest adventure in my post-divorced crazy life.

15
Looking for Razor Wire

John and I eventually began to talk on the phone as well as write. The first time he called me, I was in San Antonio, sitting on the Riverwalk sipping a piña colada. If you've never had the pleasure of receiving a call from a prison, it is strange. During the process of connecting, you're warned your conversations are monitored and recorded, and the calls are timed for a maximum of thirty minutes for which either the prisoner or the person he or she calls is charged approximately $9.00.

It's interesting, but I had never given much thought to the plight of the incarcerated, always assuming the riff-raff of society got what they deserved. But now that I was convinced that this one man was wrongfully imprisoned, I started to consider that there might be others as well or that even people who were rightfully incarcerated should have the opportunity to talk to their loved ones without having to mortgage the house. On behalf of prisoners everywhere, the cost to make a single phone call is highway robbery.

While I can't remember the specifics of the phone call, I will never forget hearing John's voice the first time. My kiddie-pool kicked in immediately when I heard the slight Texas drawl on the other end with just enough bass to curl my toes. And when I admitted to being a sucker for a deep voice, he lowered it another octave just to make sure my toes weren't the only thing curling.

I also remember the backdrop. I was staying at the Omni La Mansión del Rio, sitting in their outdoor patio right next to the water. It was a beautiful fall night and the twinkle lights were lit up and down the Riverwalk. It was the perfect setting to share with someone special – even if we were sharing it hundreds of miles apart.

After four months of writing and talking to John, he was starting to hint he was falling in love, but I was a little more reserved. I convinced myself I could not possibly be in love with someone unless it was in person, so I announced to Tammy I wanted us to take a girls' trip to Kansas to meet her brother. She agreed, and we made plans, but at the last minute, she had a death in the family and had to back out. I made the decision to go alone – I had to see in person the man I was inevitably falling for. John is incarcerated in the United States Disciplinary Barracks (USDB) on the Fort Leavenworth military base in Kansas.

The old prison was referred to as "The Castle" because its high brick walls and guard towers give it the appearance of something medieval. The new prison, which houses only males, has a much more modern feel, but there is no mistaking it is a maximum-security facility. The benefit of the military prison versus a federal prison is the inmates come with military training and most with some degree of discipline, and with rare exception, they are not career criminals.

Tammy had told me what to expect before I arrived. The inmates wear brown shirts and pants reminiscent of UPS drivers. The visitation room looks somewhat like a cafeteria. You can choose to sit around tables (designed for four) or just in plastic chairs that are separated by low plastic coffee tables. There is a drink machine and a snack machine in the room, but the visitor has to bring quarters or dollar bills for the machine as the inmates are not allowed to handle money.

The facility is located near the back of the base, and to get to it, you drive through beautiful tree-lined lanes with a magnificent view of the winding Missouri River and its bluffs in the background. It is a gorgeous drive, and my first visit to this place coincided with the changing of the leaves from green to brilliant autumn colors. The giant oaks, maples, and pecans stood in stark juxtaposition to the cold utilitarian building I would be visiting.

The base is quite expansive, and I actually thought I got lost looking for the USDB for the first time. I phoned Tammy in a bit of a panic and tried to describe my surroundings so she could get me back on track. It hadn't dawned on me prior to the trip that once on the base, GPS would not navigate me to specific installations for obvious security reasons.

Tammy did her best to try to figure out where I was, but I could only tell her I had already passed The Castle and saw railroad tracks and the river to my right. Finally, when I passed a firing range, she felt sure I was still on the right road and told me to keep going. The speed limit is 15, which made the trek to the back of the base seem even longer than it actually is. Finally, I said to Tammy the words I never dreamed I'd ever utter: "Thank goodness, I see razor wire!"

Although Tammy had prepped me, my first time to enter the visitation room was unnerving. You have to have a background check and get a pass to get through the security gates of the base. When you arrive at the prison, you have to check in again. You must have been put on a list of visitors by the inmate prior to your arrival. That process had also gone through some sort of scrutiny I wasn't privileged to. At the desk, you show two forms of photo identification and put any extraneous items in a locker, including any jackets, scarves, or hats. You can bring a small clear bag with change for the vending machines into the visitation room, as well as approved photos. Of course, cell phones or just about anything else are not allowed.

You proceed through a metal detector and a personal body check with a wand if you set off the beep, which my belt buckle or some other ornamentation invariably did. You are then buzzed into a set of double doors – the second will not open until the first is locked behind you. When the lock on the second door clicks, you can open it and seat yourself in the visitor's area and wait for the inmate to join you from an entrance opposite of the one you just came through. Nighttime visits last two and a half hours. On Saturdays and Sundays, there are two three-hour visitation sessions. I had arrived on a Thursday and planned to stay in Kansas until Sunday afternoon. If all went well, that meant five visitation sessions that would accumulate to thirteen and a half hours.

By the time I chose a seat near a narrow window with a clear view of razor wire, I was more than a little anxious. It was a weekday night, and there were very few visitors. The cafeteria that could easily seat sixty probably only had four or five people in it, including the ever-watchful guard who sat at a desk about twenty-feet away from where I sat. When John walked into the room, I drew in a breath and sized him up.

The man I had been corresponding with for four months I had never met in person; I wasn't even sure I would recognize him – or he would recognize me. But the chiseled, 6'0" cleanly-shaved, brown-clad inmate flashed a big smile, and I was immediately drawn in.
He gave me a long bear hug and asked with a bit of surprise in his voice, "Are you shaking?" I was – from head to toe – shaking like a leaf. I told him to just hold me for a second and my nerves would calm down. He hugged a little tighter before he stepped back to gauge my reaction and then decided to go in for a kiss. I didn't hesitate to meet him halfway. At that point, I already felt like I had known him my entire life.

One of the things you discover in online dating is that no matter how good the other person seems on paper, you just don't know if there's real chemistry until you meet in person. We say the word "chemistry" in relationships like it's magical, but it's really science. The neurotransmitters are finicky little substances that do whatever they like without your permission. But sometimes – if you're really lucky – you meet someone and your dopamine (which makes you feel good) and oxytocin (which floods your brain during orgasm) come to the party and take it off the charts. Then your adrenaline and norepinephrine (those fight or flight inducing hormones) spike the punch causing your hands to sweat and your heart to race. And, voilà, your frontal cortex (you know, the part reserved for good judgment), along with those parts of the brain that cause negative emotion, passes out on the couch and leaves you completely unsupervised. Woo-hoo! There is instant chemistry!

When I met John in that visitation room, the chemistry we shared was more than a party – it was a downright celebration. I was hooked, and apparently so was he. He wrote right after I left:

> *Well, it's official. I told you I was in love with you, and after seeing you this weekend, you should have no reason to doubt me. When I first saw you walk in the room, you were a vision of beauty, and I felt like you were actually squeezing my heart. When I held you in my arms I had no doubt I wanted to spend the rest of my life with you. Although I may not have let on, I was extremely nervous and so worried I was going to screw up the kiss. You know the first kiss is extremely important?*
>
> *I can't put into words how special I felt our connection was, and I'm so relieved you kept showing back up for the next visit...*

It never crossed my mind that I was dating – or not dating – when it came to John. I was just following the course of my life as if it were a stream of water flowing dutifully towards the ocean. The twists and turns were a natural occurrence in the journey as much as periods of white rapids or calm pools. I was in the midst of it, so it never fully occurred to me just how strange our circumstances were.

While I can't remember everything John and I talked about those first thirteen and a half hours of getting acquainted in person, I do remember he looked me in the eye and said, "Keri, I've been in the military for nearly two decades. I've killed a lot of men in my life, but I did not kill the four I'm convicted of killing."

The interesting thing was, I didn't ask if he had. He went on to say he would never compromise his honor by admitting guilt to something he didn't do. If it became a condition for release, he was adamant he would serve out his entire sentence.

16
Screaming Like a Girl

At one point in our correspondence, I mentioned to John I was interested in writing a book that told his side of the story in the affair that sent him to prison, a side that has yet to be told. He didn't know if he would ever want such a book written; but if he did, he would want it to primarily focus on the unfair provisions of the Uniform Code of Military Justice, how soldiers give up their constitutional rights – the very rights they serve to protect – and how they can be convicted of doing their jobs or – as in John's case – of murder with only the coerced testimony of soldiers who didn't want to go to prison themselves. I did not even know someone could be convicted of killing "four men of Middle-Eastern decent" who were never named or never even reported as missing. No bodies. No victims ever identified. No forensic evidence that a crime ever took place to begin with. He assured me if he trusted anyone to tell his story, it would be me. As time passed, I took one of the stories he had shared with me early on and turned it into a prologue just in case the book ever came to fruition:

> At 0100 hours in muggy March 1992, John Hatley was the only one in his squad awake. He was pulling security on this sweltering pitch black night. Even with the infrared of his PVS5 night vision goggles, he could barely see inches in front of his face; the jungle canopy had extinguished any moonlight

that might otherwise be seen from a higher vantage point and created the illusion of being closed off from the heavens and enveloped in some sort of subterranean world.

Hatley listened intently to the growing familiar sounds of the jungle – insects, birds, an occasional howler monkey, which the men referred to as a Bruce Lee monkey. The male katydids, with their incessant mating ritual of rubbing their wings together to attract females, gave away their locations and put themselves on the menu. A cocktail of sex and death, it was nothing short of sheer luck for the male bush cricket as to whether a female would arrive to accept his sperm or hungry bat to devour him in the night's feeding frenzy.

At twenty-two, Hatley was in his 3rd year of the infantry. His squad had been sent to Panama for Jungle Operations Training (JOT) and had established a patrol base. They were waiting to move into position for an ambush of "enemy" forces that were expected to cross the Chagres River after daylight. The Chagres was the largest river in the Panama Canal watershed, and this area of the river was surrounded by nearly impassable rainforest – a natural defense of the canal that proved superior to most human efforts. Being nearly unscathed by human interference, the area was remarkably primitive, where even in this modern 21st century native Central American plant and animal species could be observed in their natural habitat.

He was the lone soldier awake in the midst of a dark jungle teeming with life. Although he tried to put the thought out of his mind, he couldn't help but worry that lurking on every side was some creature *that wanted to devour him. In this obscure locale, he had a new respect for the veterans of Vietnam who faced perils beyond a human enemy. He was well aware a fer-de-lance, bushmaster, or tree viper could be lurking underfoot or slithering up a tree. And while he wasn't particularly afraid of spiders, he also knew Central America was home to the world's smallest spider, the world's largest spider, and some of the world's deadliest spiders. The Wandering Spider, which actually hunkered down at night, could easily find refuge in human clothing, bedding, or the log upon which he was sitting. These spiders did not demonstrate typical arachnid behavior and hide if frightened.*

On the contrary, they were quite aggressive and known to stand their ground by raising their fore-legs and readying the pincher-like claws near their mouth for an attack. They were fast and venomous and impossible to detect in this dark, crawling world. And the small creatures were not to be outdone by the larger ones. Puma and jaguar hunted these jungles at night. Yep, his mind couldn't help but think that everything around him was lethal and ready to pounce.

The young private had joined the infantry October 26, 1989. His Baptist-preacher father had instilled in him the belief that every American male owed three years of his life to the military. Hatley patriotism was unwavering, and John would be one of many Hatley men, including his grandfather, to give back to the country he loved and respected. His father had tried to enlist as well but did not meet the minimum weight requirements. The younger Hatley had no such issues. At 6' and 215 pounds, his stature never came into question. He recalled the day he went to enlist. Pop had told him, "Son, whatever you do, don't sign up for the infantry. They're going to tell you that's all they've got, but it isn't."

John had replied, "Don't worry, Pop. I won't." When he returned several hours later, newly enlisted in the Armed Forces, Hatley senior asked in what branch had he enlisted.

"Infantry," John replied.

His father's only comment was, "Well, I don't want to hear you sniveling and whining about it six months from now." Hatley never forgot those words, and he never sniveled or whined in spite of the path he would endure, a path he could not fathom at this moment.

Hatley detected movement outside of the perimeter. He strained in the darkness to make out the source of the disturbance. Although barely audible he detected the parting of grasses and the crunching of leaves that could have come from any one of the nearly ninety species native to the area. His instinct told him it was not a single entity moving towards him. His mind quickly gave a narrative to the sensory input, and he whispered to a sleeping Sergeant Stevens, "Sergeant, wake up. I think the enemy is coming."

Hatley's anxiety increased as he realized whoever or whatever was coming towards the patrol was moving much faster. He leaned back behind the log to shake the still-sleeping Sergeant, knowing they had little time to wake the others and defend themselves, and at that moment the full assault began. A band of thirty to forty creatures overran the camp of sleeping soldiers who sprang to bewildered wakefulness and reaction.

Hatley screamed like a girl as one of the small beasts leapt up and planted its hind legs into his chest. He fell backward and rolled over the log, holding on to his M-249 as he struggled to figure out the nature of the attack. In the chaos, Stevens picked up a squad automatic weapon, loaded with blanks for the training operations, and started shooting at the nocturnal enemy combatants who were leaping through the camp and bouncing over startled soldiers. Between the gunfire and creature contact, chaos ensued.

Somewhere in the foray, to Hatley's chagrin, the realization came that the band of white-nosed coatimundi, a medium-sized mammal that looks like the bastard offspring of a monkey and raccoon, were only a disturbance and not a threat. Nocturnal foraging is a common activity for these Panama natives, but being on the move in such a hurry probably meant the band had been spooked by a predator.

In the end, the company erupted in delirious laughter – they had all panicked; none of them manned-up or showed the copious amounts of testosterone each believed he possessed. There were no human heroes that came forth to squelch the coati raid. The small creatures that had no idea they were even engaged in a skirmish were the only ones to save face that night.

For most, this experience would have been a Baptism in humiliation, but Hatley was different. He had uncommon buoyancy, balanced by a knack for self-deprecating humor. He knew how to laugh – at himself, at others, at situations. Although earnest

> about his service, everything else could be chalked up to a learning experience that just might come in handy somewhere down the road.
>
> The men jeered him throughout the rest of the operation, "Wasn't that Hatley screaming like a girl?" Hatley offered plausible deniability – weren't they all screaming like girls? No one could be sure he was the only one.

John, like his sister, is eternally optimistic and positive. He just makes the best of his situation and moves forward. He has used his time in prison to get first a Bachelor's degree and was now working on his Master's. Visiting him at the USDB was more fun than I could have imagined. He is charming and charismatic with a side of incorrigible humor. He is also a self-proclaimed habitual line stepper and completely uninhibited. At times he has to be reminded to tone down his language and crassness for the general population. He is never short on stories or jokes, but he likes to listen as well. From the beginning, I felt he genuinely wanted to know everything about me that I was willing to share.

Before the chemical reaction I experienced at the USDB, I didn't believe in love at first sight. In fact, I was almost to the point I no longer believed in romantic love at all. The only unrelated man I could absolutely say I loved was Alex, and although sometimes the lines between Philia and Eros blurred, it had finally become abundantly clear he was like a brother to me. John was different and seemed to embody my ideal soul mate – except for the annoying fact he was in prison. Two months after my visit, for Christmas, he had a print made for my wall. It was a translated quote from the opera *Falstaff* by Verdi centered in a double panel floating wall mount with a black frame around it:

> *When I saw you, I fell in love, and you smiled because you knew.*

He was not alone in that sentiment. Within seconds of our first meeting at the USDB, I could cross off the twenty-third item on my bucket list, "falling in love at first sight."

In searching for the perfect Christmas gift for John, I contacted one of his favorite authors, Diana Gabaldon. We were both fans of the *Outlander* series of novels and even felt some sort of connection to the passionate protagonists who transcended time to be together. John and I frequently closed our letters with a sentiment that expressed loving completely and beyond just this existence, "Both our hearts, all our lives." When I wrote to Ms. Gabaldon and shared our story, to my surprise and delight, she was magnanimous and accommodating. Three days before Christmas, a 20th Anniversary Edition of *Outlander* showed up on my doorstep with the inscription:

> *To John, a modern-day Jamie who found his Claire in Keri. May both of your hearts be full...all of your lives. Diana Gabaldon*

After I returned from Leavenworth, John and I continued to grow our relationship through phone calls and correspondence. I stopped worrying about the confines of a long-distance relationship and just allowed myself to really be in love with him, odd circumstances and restrictions be damned.

John embodied so many of the characteristics I find attractive: a man who is rugged, strong, a protector of the weak, brave. I was also drawn to his intellect and communication skills.

He had already proven he could expound on a wide variety of topics. He displayed wit and sarcasm, which were additional markers of intelligence as far as I was concerned. He reminded me of a Renaissance man – a man who can fight on a battlefield and still recite poetry to his girl, a man who is at home in the wilderness yet can navigate the city scene, a man with primitive instinct but refined mannerisms.

Okay, maybe his mannerisms would need a little polishing once he was released, but he fit the dichotomy I was looking for. Fatigues or a tux – he embodied both archetypes.

It's hard to explain why I fell so quickly and completely for John and just jumped into the abyss without giving much thought to how this relationship might ultimately turn out. In my defense, I had known members of his family for years, and I was very much acquainted with his career. The man locked in Leavenworth was also the hometown hero, and many people in our community had fought to get him released. Coincidentally, even I had written a letter of support during the trial eight years ago.

John's words echoed my own sentiments:

Keri,

I just don't seem to be able to stop thinking about you. I hope you're doing wonderfully. Do you have any idea the restraint I have shown not to pick up the phone and call you every day? I want you to know if I had my way, I'd be calling you constantly. What can I say? I just love to hear your voice. You have the sweetest laugh. Every time I hear it, I can't help but smile. You're just so perfect that sometimes it doesn't seem real. I can't help but include you in every plan I make for the future. Are you okay with that? Although it pains me to think of the hurt you've experienced while going through your divorce, I am ecstatic your ex was such a fool. I fully intend to capitalize on his idiocy. That's right! I have no shame! Lol! It's so much more than falling in love with you. You are everything I have ever imagined a woman to be. I feel as though this void in my heart is finally filling. The feelings I have for you are unbound by traditional reason, and I find myself uncontrollably surrendering my heart to you...

The letters and conversations were not all hearts and roses but continued to have substance as we revealed our faults and quirks and the negative aspects of our personalities and experiences. For me, it was confessing the insecurities from the divorce and living with the Narcissist for thirty years and sharing some of the toughest moments that led to the final breakup.

For him, it was revealing the realities of being a soldier for two decades. He had witnessed and partaken in the horrors of more than one war. Soldiers are trained to eliminate the threat; he was good at it and unapologetic for it. I could tell he was careful to reveal his darkest memories gently so as not to shock me with the life he had lived. In one letter he said it was one thing when adults suffered, but it was altogether different when it was children. He talked in generalities about the failed rescue of two Iraqi boys who had been kidnapped. Although he and his men were able to catch the kidnappers, they arrived fifteen to twenty minutes too late to save the boys from horrific demise. I couldn't truly fathom all he had been exposed to on foreign battlefields, but I knew it had shaken his belief system to the core and taken a toll on his spirit. Strangely, I accepted all the contradictions that existed in this man. Harnessing my flare for the dramatic, I wrote in my journal:

> *I was always taught you should give wide berth to a man who possesses a dark soul, one that can kill without remorse, one that even takes pleasure in the aggression. And I did…until I met him. The warrior who traversed time to meet me in this present life seemed cognizant that his power to crush and conquer was not limited to an adversary but could unwittingly be unleashed even in love. It was as if he knew the darkness if revealed in one fell swoop would frighten and destroy any chance he had at a union with my lighter soul.*
>
> *So with calculated discernment and gentleness, he began to disclose the layers and start the descent into the murky recesses of his being, nursing me only to the point of nausea and then providing soothing antidote before I could vomit, little by little building my tolerance for vitriol.*
>
> *Only I was more aware than he knew of the man before me – who he is and of what he is capable. I know his hands have dealt sordid judgment and exhausted breath. I know his mind has calculated and exacted strategy to bring about human demise. I know his eyes have registered the horror and final*

moments of one in his grip, and his flesh has imbibed in their warm, freshly splattered blood. I know he is dangerous.

But the paradox of this man who both revels in malevolence and loves with unbridled passion and commits with unparalleled allegiance is an allure I cannot withstand. For those same hands that exhaust life exude tender caress; the mind that calculates demise for his enemy plots to elevate me to the sublime; those eyes that witness untold carnage see through my imperfections with perfecting clarity; that flesh that knows spilt blood heats me to the core.

And while he embraces his own blackness and is satisfied to ascend into the abyss, I see the divergent embers waiting to be fanned and consume the darkness with brilliant firelight.

It is those embers of honor, selflessness, passion, acumen, and fearlessness that square the necessary attributes of iniquity a hero must possess to wage relentless war on his foes and emerge the victor.

To occupy and illuminate the heart of such a man is a rarity not often bestowed on mere mortals.

Our correspondence alternated between playful and serious, and we both questioned each other relentlessly. Our quest for information about the other person seemed insatiable. We wrote so often and such lengthy letters that we both worried the other might see us as a stalker. When we finally made this mutual confession, he offered to hire me in Ramen noodles to continue to stalk him as proof he wasn't a bit bothered by the sheer volume of mail. In all, John wrote me 219 letters over the next year and a half, and I wrote him 173, not counting the holiday and "just because" cards I would send. It was a conundrum even to me that I felt like I knew this man like the back of my hand, but I had never seen him in a color other than brown. We expected he would probably be released in August. Even though he told me not to get my hopes up, I set a countdown clock on my computer and went on with life, waiting both patiently and impatiently for that event happen. It just seemed a natural part of God's charge for me to be still and my propensity not to.

17
Brown Corduroy Pants

It might seem a little dismal to carry on a relationship with such severe limitations, but John and I both know how to have fun and make the best of any situation. We were never short on topics to discuss, and we never stopped learning about the other person. Once on the phone, John claimed he could tell if I was embarrassed or blushing just by the sound of my voice, and he said I would never make a good poker player because I had no bluff. My tells were too easy. Unbeknownst to him, I took that as a challenge to make up a story and convince him it was the total truth. I had no desire to be so easily read.

From the beginning, John and I had talked about how he would like to dress when he got out. After years in military fatigues followed by more years in prison brown, he had little opportunity to dress for his own personal taste. He told me he would probably wear pearl snaps, jeans, and boots. He felt sure he would buy all his shirts at a feed store or a Tractor Supply. I was a little taken aback and mentioned that perhaps he might like a nice dress shirt from a menswear store that sported buttons instead of snaps. It was easy to see our tastes were going to clash.

I knew this would make perfect fodder to use to pull off the lie.

A few weeks later, after I was sure he had forgotten the bluff conversation, I got a call from John. In a very excited tone, I told him I had been to the mall and picked out an outfit for him to wear home when he was released. I could hear the hesitation in his voice. He didn't want to hurt my feelings or quell my enthusiasm, but he was pretty sure he would not like anything I had picked out, especially if it came from a store in the mall.

I told him, "John, don't worry. I have excellent taste in men's clothing. Just hear me out before you judge."

He got a little more worried. He really loved me, but I'm sure he felt like we were about to have our first fight. I continued, "Since you've been locked up, styles for men have changed a little. Lots of men wear pants with narrow ankles and deck shoes. I saw the coolest brown corduroy pants today. Now don't freak; I know you don't like brown, but this is a really cool shade of brown..."

He interrupted, "Keri, did you say corduroy? I don't wear corduroy. Not going to happen."

I was cracking up on the inside, but I kept my voice as serious as ever. I also acted just a little bit like he was hurting my feelings to make the lie even more convincing. "John, I promise you I know what I'm talking about. I would never put you in anything unflattering. These brown corduroy pants are quite popular and extremely flattering. I got them on sale, and I can't take them back."

He commenced an awkward long pause and drew in a deep breath. I could tell he was trying so hard not to sound angry or bullheaded, "Sweetheart, I just don't wear corduroy. Ever." He said "ever" with unmistakable emphasis and at least one octave lower than every other word in that sentence.

I was relentless, and in my sweetest tone, I

continued, "But you'll love them. I promise. Just give them a chance." And the coup de grâce, "For me."

He couldn't take anymore but knew he wasn't going to be able to spare my feelings. He declared sternly, "Keri, I'm serious. I will not wear them."

I won! I started laughing and said, "You thought I couldn't bluff you, huh?"

He was so relieved that I really didn't expect him to wear brown corduroy pants that it escaped him for a moment I could lie straight up, and he couldn't detect it at all. His only come back was, "Well, yeah, over the phone. In person, you'd never be able to keep a straight face."

He didn't realize he had just laid a new gauntlet, and I had accepted the challenge the very moment he told me there was something I couldn't do – even if that something was lying with a straight face while looking him in the eye.

Again, I waited months. It was St. Patrick's day when I was visiting John in Kansas that I set out to prove I could bald-faced lie and not give it away with red cheeks or a silly grin. I visited first on a Friday night. He asked what I was going to do when I left, and I told him I had seen an Irish Pub I thought about checking out. I was hungry and could get some dinner and maybe have a drink or two.

The next morning at visitation he inquired about my night, and I told him I was sitting alone at the pub when a group of five or six men and women invited me to join them at their table. They were concerned that anyone would be alone on St. Paddy's day. When I told them why my boyfriend wasn't with me, they empathized with my plight and included me in their festivities. John initially reacted as if he was glad I had not been bored and alone. I told him I shot darts and played pool with them and then went back to my hotel room. And I mentioned, by the way, that they had invited me to a private party they were having that night at one of their homes. They said I should come by when visitation was over. I even pretended to have an address.

Since I met John, he had always been a little concerned about my lackadaisical approach to personal safety, but he also knew I wasn't one to be bossed around. After my marriage ended, I had no intention of ever being with a my-way-or-the-highway man again. So John was always sure to tread lightly when trying to "encourage" me to be just a little more cautious. He commented as nonchalantly as possible, "Well, it's nice that you had people to hang out with last night, but you're not going to actually go to some stranger's house, are you?"

I replied casually, "Probably not. I don't know. We'll see."

Then I changed the topic. Several times he tried to go back to it, "I'm not telling you what to do, but you really have no idea who these people are. How many men did you say were in the group?"

Again, I dismissed his concerns and replied coolly, "It was about even men and women, I think. I'm not sure. Yeah, I probably won't go."

I wouldn't give him the definitive "of course, I'm not going" that he wanted to hear. He couldn't let it go and kept returning to the topic with a slightly different approach each time. My flippant dismissals were making him crazy, and I could see his face start to turn red. We kept this banter up until I completely exasperated him, and he blurted out, "Look, I don't want you going over to some stranger's house where there might be a bunch of guys who either want to hook up or worse!"

I calmly reassured him, "John, it's fine. I met these guys last night. They are all really nice."

"I don't care, Keri. This is not okay with me!"

I had him, "John, they were just a bunch of normal guys, drinking green beer and wearing corduroy pants and having a good time."

He missed it at first, "Keri, you have no idea what these guys are like...did you say corduroy pants?"

"Yes, John. They were all wearing brown corduroy pants. Gotcha!"

When he realized what I had done and how well I pulled it off, he was more than a little impressed and amused. We both had a good belly laugh. Of course, he then pointed out I was priding myself on the fact I could lie to him with a straight face. Come to think of it, was that really a win? Regardless, "brown corduroy pants" became a code between the two of us whenever we might be pulling the other's leg.

18
The Second Law of Thermodynamics

And my love life continued to paradoxically progress and be stuck in the confines of Leavenworth. While on another playing field of my life, I was undergoing a completely different rumination.

While reading about The Second Law of Thermodynamics: *the entropy of a closed system will never decrease*, I considered the whole of my current situation and the truths in the disorder of this thing we call life. I was more than aware that life without effort will dissolve into chaos, and I vaguely felt that I had been grasping and clawing to prevent that very outcome, especially in the profession to which I had never questioned my devotion. Without nurture, however, all things deteriorate – love deteriorates, work deteriorates, life deteriorates.

There is a television series called, "Life After People," in which scientists, engineers, and other experts speculate on what would happen to Earth if people no longer occupied it. They would usually take a well-known landmark or historical site and use computer animation to reveal what would inevitably be deterioration and ruin. Of course, they would delve into a dramatic explanation of the process – things like oxidation compromising steel structures, previously domesticated animals returning feral, unchecked growth of weeds and fauna.

Too many demands had caused me to be somewhat absentia in the important arenas of my life, and for too long I had allowed my career to take center stage. Suddenly, the Second Law of Thermodynamics was real to me, and I did not desire metaphorical urban decay to gain foothold in areas I deemed as priority and focus. There were people and situations that needed my attention, and it was important to nurture that which I wanted to keep fresh and youthful. My family, specifically my children and grandchildren, craved for me to be present and powerful. And while John did not need me, per se, he desired me, and that was all the more reason to place emphasis on fueling and cultivating the relationship. What better reason to retire from a career that had grown tedious and churlish? Not because I was old or tired, but because I was invigorated to pour my labors into creating higher art. I was resolved, and my decision to retire became one to purge my life of the refuse that was zapping my energy and causing me to be less than I should be. Thus, I began the process which would take a little over six months.

In wrapping things up on the work front, I eventually cut my hours to half time, which was more conducive to trips to Leavenworth. I could usually fit four to six visitation sessions into each trip, and little by little that became my new norm. The house he was going to build became the house we wanted to build together. He allowed my input, and we sent the plans back and forth to each other until we perfected our dream home. In spite of the unusual, bordering ridiculous, circumstances, I never doubted the relationship.

Several of my trips to Kansas were noteworthy beyond just getting to visit with John. One, in particular, centered around a celestial event, and I can never resist a remarkable happening in the heavens. Parts of Kansas fell in that narrow seventy-mile band across the United States where the eclipse of the sun would reach totality. In Leavenworth, for one minute and thirty-one seconds. I made a point to be there. I joined a group of people sitting in a military cemetery on the side of a hill. The handful of us were not only star-gazers, but we had a special connection to veterans in one way or another. The couple to my left was a Vietnam veteran and his wife. They asked why I was in Kansas alone, and I told them my story. It turned out they had known of John's plight almost since its inception and had been praying for his release. I never cease to be amazed at just how small the world is when you take a few minutes to pay attention. I was on the phone with John during the eclipse, and we shared that moment of unnatural darkness together, juxtaposition for the bright future we imagined to be right around the corner.

However, in mid-October things took a dramatically different turn when John would finally get the news he had waited for since August. Both the parole board in Leavenworth and the board in D.C. recommended John's release, but it was vetoed by the Deputy Assistant to the Secretary of the Army. It was an unexpected and devastating blow, and it was the beginning of the end of our relationship.

I worried instantly John would push me away. I figured now that his release was uncertain instead of imminent he would not want me to wait for him indefinitely. There were some other problems creeping up between us as well – problems that were enhanced by the limitations of imprisonment. He was frustrated by my relationship with my ex, and although I had gotten better at setting boundaries, there were still some issues. He had always been a little jealous of my friendship with Alex, but now a woman from John's past had come into the picture, and it was my turn to be jealous. She began to visit him frequently, and whether he could see it or not, I knew she was interested in more than just friendship. It is difficult to say what happened exactly, but we had both fallen so hard and fast that we had ignored the reality that John might have to serve out his full term – nearly another ten years. The parole veto instantly sobered John, and he wrestled with the demons of a future that was entirely at the mercy of the Army who made it clear that John would have to confess before he would be released. We broke up for a week, but we were both miserable and got back together quickly. However, something was still off, and six weeks later, John broke it off with me permanently, claiming he loved me but we were too different and he was no longer sure about us or his future in general.

The unexpected phone call was devastating. While it was a long conversation with tears and explanation, I just remember that he said he was no longer sure he was "all in," to which I replied, "Well, if you're not all in, I'm out." I hung up the phone at a complete loss. Three days later, my retirement was official. Suddenly, everything in my life had changed. My career of thirty years had ended, and the primary relationship I wanted to put all my energy into was gone.

I believed John to be my soul mate – and there could only be one in the universe. If I had found my soul mate and it didn't work out, then what was left to find?

Part 3: Life After Love

19
The Break-up Template

After a long period of intensely mourning my break up with John, going through the stages of grief as if someone had died, leaning on God, family, and friends for emotional survival – I finally put on my big-girl panties, wiped the mascara out from under my eyes, and resumed my journey to the center of the online dating earth. If I had found love once, I reasoned, I could find it again.

I reinstated my profile, this time trying out a site that appealed to country folks, specifically farmers. Now, I am not a farmer, but they boast on their site that you don't have to be a farmer to join. I was just looking for someone really genuine, and this site seemed to offer that. Besides, my daughter thought their commercials were hilarious. She mimicked the catch phrase to me, "City folks just don't get it."

You can always tell who has been on a dating site for a while. There are some tell-tale statements in their undoubtedly-revised profiles:

- *No serial daters.*
- *If you're not willing to actually go on a date, why are you on a dating website?*
- *No drama.*
- *I do not respond if your profile doesn't include a picture.*
- *Please be sure your pictures are recent.*

The necessity for people to include these phrases in their profiles surprised me at first. I mean, is there anyone out there, for instance, who wants drama? I was also puzzled by the frequency of the "no serial daters" phrase. While I felt like I knew what it probably meant, I couldn't fathom why it was important enough to include in a profile that you knew you had to keep to a minimum if you wanted it to be read in its entirety.

After a few failed first dates, I quickly remembered setting up a date and going on it was the easy part. Actually finding someone you connected enough with to go on a second or third date was the difficult part. At least for me. In fact, I had so many "one and done" dates (as I affectionately began calling them) that my now teenaged daughter suggested I have a breakup template. I kid you not.

Here's the deal, I live in a small rural town. I have to drive at least forty-five minutes to do just about anything – shop at a department store, go to the movies, eat at a large chain restaurant, etc. And while I'm not the best driver on the planet – my apologies to the mailbox I hit last week – I do not text and drive. So when my daughter is with me, and I hear that familiar bamboo tap, she quickly grabs my phone and announces I have a text and who it is from. She will usually read the text to me and ask how I want to respond. I always enjoyed having my little personal secretary taking care of these minor details for me; however, I will admit there have been a few awkward times when I've had to explain to the child what she just read and try to minimize any life-long scarring that might take place.

So one day we were making our typical drive to the big town, and I got a text from the guy I had gone out with the weekend before. My daughter asked how I wanted to reply, and I answered, "I don't know. I don't plan to go out with him again."

The wiser of the two of us then said matter-of-factly, "Mom, you need a break-up template."

What? I was quickly taken aback, but the sage continued, "You know, Mom: 'Dear (insert name here), Thank you for our date at (insert place here). I had a really nice time and enjoyed meeting you. You are a very (insert positive descriptive adjective here) man, but I don't feel like we have a connection. I wish you the best of luck on your search to find true love.'"

At this point I was giggling – not only did it sound very similar to the many "there will be no second date" texts I had actually sent, but it was obvious she got her love of grammar from me. Those were her words, including the "descriptive adjective" part. After I got over laughing at my daughter and myself, a horrible thought occurred to me, "Am I a serial dater?"

I was so mortified at the supposition of being a serial dater, I began to quiz my friends. Almost unanimously, they told me they think a serial dater is a reference to a woman who just wants to go out to get a free meal or movie, and it's not meant to chastise someone who is truly looking for a real connection. I know I'm willing to go Dutch on dates, and I've often paid for the activity, such as a movie, if my date bought the meal or vice versa. Still, by the sheer volume of my one-and-done dates, I was a little shaken and introspective.

I have a theory on why this is occurring. In a "normal" – is that even a thing anymore? – dating situation, you know someone before they ask you out.

You work together or go to church together or play on the same softball league – something. You have an idea of what the person is like in a social setting. You already know if his mannerisms make you cringe or if his voice grates on your nerves like fingernails screeching down a chalkboard. You're likely aware of his interactions with people and know whether he kicks dogs or makes babies cry. You already don't care if he's bald and doesn't groom his nose hairs – or maybe you do – but the point is online dating is only one-step removed from blind dating. You have so much to discover about someone that I believe the odds of having a connection are stacked against you.

There is a show I've watched a few seasons of called "Married at First Sight," where, true to its title, complete strangers agree to get married when they meet at the altar. Couples are matched by a team of experts: a psychologist, a sociologist, a sexologist (yes, this is an actual job), and a humanist chaplain.

The premise is that these experts lead a diligent search process that involves psychological and background evaluations, batteries of personality tests, face-to-face interviews, and ultimately (for about 100-200 candidates) evaluative workshops. The final few candidates even get a home visit by the psychologist.

As a divorced woman in my fifties who was engaged in online dating, I watched the show out of some sort of morbid curiosity, the proverbial train wreck I couldn't help but see myself in. Obviously, I was finding it very difficult to find the perfect match on my own, and I was curious to see if the experts could do it better – if maybe there was some scientific formula that was superior at picking out a suitable partner for you than you could do for yourself.

The idea was entertaining. I was also really curious about how much money you could earn as a sexologist and just exactly what are the credentials for such a job? (In hindsight, it just seems so much more entertaining than grading English compositions written by moderately engaged high school students, which I had done for nineteen years.)

In each season of "Married at First Sight," the show matches three couples. Viewers get to follow these couples from the marriage ceremony to the wedding night to the honeymoon to moving in together for six weeks. At the end of six weeks, these couples make a decision to stay married or get divorced.

They have a lot at stake. They agree to a legally-binding marriage and must go through a divorce if the experiment fails and they decide they are not compatible and don't fall in love.

There's so much going on here, that it's hard to break down. First of all, is love a choice? Under the right circumstances do you actually make a cognitive decision to be in love, or is there something beyond our ability to control or understand that connects us to another individual – like the science of chemistry I had experienced at Leavenworth? I was curious to see if the experts could do a better job matching strangers than I seemed to be doing in finding a match for myself.

At first, I thought there might be something to it. Four of the first six couples agreed to stay married at the end of the six-week period. The experts seemed to be doing a pretty good job! However, a few years later, only two couples remained married. The next six couples had an even higher divorce rate, with three initially agreeing to stay married, but all six being divorced shortly afterward. Unfortunately, the experts didn't seem to have a magic – or rather scientific – potion either. I might as well throw that application to "Married at First Sight" in the garbage and stick to online dating.

20
Not Exactly a Joy Ride

The profile hadn't been up long when Martin sent me a message. Although he lived in the same state, the drive would be a good five or six hours, so I responded, "Thank you for your interest, but I feel the distance is too far for dating, and I'm tied to the area I live in." Since I thought that settled the matter, I was surprised by Martin's persistence in wanting to correspond and insistence that the drive was no problem for him as he was not tied to any area. He then sent a message asking if we could talk on the phone because he preferred that mode of communication.

I have since added to the list of things to engage the dating "Spidey" senses: *wanting to exchange numbers too quickly without establishing at least some commonalities via messaging.*

But at the time, I agreed to a phone call more out of curiosity than anything else. Once Martin had me on the phone, he began a diatribe relating his life story. It turns out, he's a truck driver, and I live near his route destination, so he's in the area quite frequently. That assuaged my curiosity about the distance.

To be honest, Martin seemed like a man in pain. His divorce had been recent, and I could tell he seemed lonely – even perhaps a little desperate, and that engaged my empathy, so I talked to him longer than I should have. In the course of the hour-long conversation, he made the statement that his marriage broke up when his wife "stopped doing what she was told."

Pump the brakes! I interrupted Martin at that point to remind him this is the 21st century, and women are not subservient housekeepers to be kept in their places. I told him I was sorry for his pain, but we would not be a good match at all. Case closed! Or so I thought.

Have you ever seen the movie, "Joy Ride," were these teens pull a prank on a lonely truck driver who turns out to be a psychotic murderer? Upon hanging up, I started to get a creepy feeling that maybe I had entertained the wrong person – if even just for an hour phone conversation. Martin texted me the next morning. (If you know anything about my personality, one of my character flaws is putting up with bullshit for too long. Hence a thirty-year marriage to a Narcissistic asshole.)

I should have simply blocked Martin's number right away, but being empathetic to the man's lonely plight, I responded and explained again that regardless of whether or not I misinterpreted his misogynist comment, I was not interested in dating him. I wished him the best of luck in finding someone who was. As soon as I texted, the phone rang. How quickly I had forgotten Martin's preferred method of communication!

When I answered, he was initially apologetic for the statement he made and tried to tell me how I had taken his comment the wrong way. I tried a different route, reassuring him that all was well, that there was no need to apologize, and that we were just different people. I told him yet again I wished him luck in finding someone on the site. He wouldn't let it go, and then things took a turn for the weird.

Martin, with increasing anger that I wasn't seeing things his way, made a statement that he was interested in dating me exclusively. WHAT? He didn't even know me outside of our hour on the phone. I have enough confidence to think I'm a decent catch, but trust me, there is nothing about me so special that a man should give up the pursuit of all other women after a single phone call. As much as I might like to think it, I'm just not that spectacular. Something else had to be going on here, and that something was adding up to be that Martin was an angry person and perhaps a crazy stalker.

Do you know that feeling you get in your gut about something? Being instantly able to make a judgment with very limited information? Social psychologist Malcolm Gladwell writes about the phenomena of thin-slicing. He posits it's not your gut at all, but your brain in just nanoseconds forms a sort of template based on your past experiences and knowledge in any given situation to create a swift subconscious analysis. The brain doesn't have time to explain it to you, so it just sends you a quick signal so you can react or "get a feeling" about something. Apparently, thin-slicing can be very accurate. (My apologies to Mr. Gladwell in advance for doing such a poor job of relating the idea he so eloquently explains, but I would encourage you to read *Blink: The Power of Thinking Without Thinking*. He does a much better job, and it's a really insightful read.)

My point is, I should have paid closer attention to my thin-slicing that very first conversation. I knew just a few minutes into it there was something about Martin that didn't feel quite right. Stuck on the phone a second time, I switched tactics again and was now trying to convince Martin that I was more than not a good fit – hell, I was telling him I wasn't even a good catch. However, Martin seemed to know more about me than I had divulged. To my growing concern, I realized this man had done some cyber-stalking in the fourteen hours since I last spoke to him. Apparently, my married surname (which I was still using at the time) was uncommon enough that with just a little bit of additional information, like how to spell it properly, my large digital footprint was easy to locate.

Martin begged to come and see me or at least meet me at a restaurant near where I lived, and he rationalized why I should give him a second consideration. But all I wanted to do at this point was to get off the phone with a reasonable assurance I would not hear air brakes pulling up in my driveway.

Over the next few weeks I lost count of the times Martin reached out to me. I never responded to the text messages or picked up the calls, but I read them and listened to the voicemails he left numerous times a day. While there were no direct threats, his persistence and insistence were downright scary. My daughter wanted to know why I didn't just block his number, and I told her because I wanted to see just how long it would take for the calls to stop. If it was a staring contest, he won – I finally broke down and blocked the number. I'm not sure how long he kept trying to reach me, but now that movie "Joy Ride" is just a little less far-fetched and a little more terrifying.

21
The Gerbil Debacle

At some point, you might think at least one of these experiences should deter me from my pursuit of a love connection, but I'm tenacious if anything. Before the divorce, we had a ball python named Lucy as a family pet. Now a ball python is smaller than the giants that get all the publicity, like the reticulated python. A ball usually grows no larger than 6-7 feet in length. In my humble opinion, their smaller size makes them better "pets" because they are less likely to be able to squeeze the life out of their owners. This was a plus as far as I was concerned. I use the term "pet" loosely when it comes to snakes. I am more than aware those wily serpents are anything but trainable. At best, they just get used to the way you smell and how you handle them, and they decide you're neither food nor a threat.

Lucy had a wonderful temperament, and by that, I only mean she had decided we were not menacing or victuals, and she didn't feel a need to waste her energy by biting us. I got her for my son when he was in the third grade because it was his eight-year-old heart's desire to own a snake; but after the novelty wore off for him, I ended up being her primary caretaker and handling her the most.

We had to feed her live gerbils because she had a food phobia and wouldn't eat anything else. Although it seemed absurd, this was actually diagnosed by an exotic animal veterinarian who cited the scars on her back as evidence. He told us her previous owner must have left live food in the cage – likely a rat – and instead of Lucy eating her meal, the meal likely chewed on Lucy's back. Apparently, rats and gerbils have slightly different smells because while Lucy was terrified of rats, gerbils were a delicacy for her. If Lucy would only eat gerbils, then that is what I was determined to feed her, and I bought them at a mom-and-pop pet store until it closed down. At that point, the only pet store left in town was part of a national chain. They didn't "sell" the animals in their store; you paid to "adopt a pet" instead.

Spoiler alert: I literally got kicked out of this PETA-friendly store for "adopting" a gerbil. After I purchased it, aka went through the pseudo-adoption process, the sales lady was trying to give me directions on how to care for the social little rodent. I explained to her there was no need since I was feeding it to my snake. I assured her it wouldn't even be needing a cage. She freaked out and started urgently summoning the manager over the loudspeaker as if I was holding a gun to her and robbing her. The manager came running over to find out what was wrong.

Meanwhile, I was trying to leave because I had already bought the damn thing. However, the zealous manager literally blocked the door and would not let me leave with the gerbil. Long story short, it was a scene. After my diatribe about the circle of life and the hypocrisy in selling omnivores but not their food, I was "permanently banned" from shopping in this particular chain ever again. Being more than just a little tenacious and slightly passive aggressive about this, I "adopted" many more gerbils from the store over the next few years. You see, I had paid cash – and they had no idea the name of the person they "banned for life" from shopping in their store. From that point on, after every adoption, I was careful to take note of how to care for the cute little gerbil at home so as not to upset any salesperson who might also happen to be a vegetarian.

Obviously, I'm not one to be easily deterred. The next guy I would talk to was Keith, who like all the others before him, looked like a really nice guy. We seemed to have some things in common, and he didn't live but an hour or so from me. We quickly switched from dating-site messaging to texting, but almost on cue, things turned strange. He started referencing himself in the third person and as "Cowboy." Daily I started receiving, "Cowboy Keith is thinking about you" or "This Cowboy sure can't wait to meet you" or "This Cowboy is feeling tired tonight." Unfortunately, or fortunately, depending on your perspective, the timing for Keith the Cowboy was not ideal.

I had just had the stalker experience with Martin, and now my thin-slicing was diaphanous and screaming "no" for reasons I couldn't put my finger on, but I listened. I let Keith know I didn't think we were a fit and moved on. My one-and-done dates had been reduced to text messaging gone wrong, and I no longer needed even a first date to be done.

22
Whopper Plopper #75

Thoreau once wrote, "Many men go fishing all their lives without knowing it is not the fish they are after." When I was younger, I did some amateur rock climbing. It's a challenging and somewhat demanding hobby. The experience for me changed my perspective on life in a major way. I remember climbing once at Enchanted rock. I checked the belay system one final time before my assent would begin. "On belay," I yelled to my partner, a colleague who was an experienced climber patiently trying to teach this beginner. "Belay on," he aptly replied.

The journey began, inch by inch. I reached over my head for the first handhold, felt the damp coolness of rock awaken my bare fingers. They gripped and a slight stinging sensation demanded a moment of attention. "Climb with your legs," he yelled from below. My foot found the first foothold about the height of my waist; my toes burned in the cramped shoe. I used my calf and thigh muscles to push, and eventually, I was midway up. I reached higher; my free foot groped for the next hold. Hand over hand, foot over foot – reaching, pushing, moving.

My focus was on the rock. Training had taught me not to look up or down but to focus on the task. The stinging in my fingers and toes were replaced by warming agility; my mind was problem-solving. Where was the next hold? What was the best route? I breathed the air – air that was somehow crisper even twenty feet off the ground. I felt the sun warming my back and the rock simultaneously. I noticed a fellow climber – a small spider that quickly scurried back into a dark crevice, a handhold I decided to avoid. At some point, I became star-fished on the rock. "Star-fished" is a climbing term for getting yourself into an overly comfortable position and not wanting to move out of it into a more difficult, less stable state. I knew it was imperative to be slightly out of balance and ready to move, so I reluctantly but determinedly gave up my nested spot and continued upward. Hand over hand, foot over foot – reaching, pushing, moving.

Finally, I arrived at the destination – the summit I had eyed an hour before. I climbed to solid ground, removed the belay system, and stood full-faced in the sun. I looked up at the sky, which I was then closer to, and down at the ground I had conquered. Thoreau is right. The fish are the destination; life is about the journey. It would have been just as simple to reach the summit through a foot trail as climb the sheer cliff – the fish available to either traveler. But it was never the fish I was after. I told myself this online dating quest was no different – I needed to stop focusing on the catch and just embrace the journey no matter how awkward or bumpy it felt at any given juncture. At least I was in no way star-fished!

At this point, my story about dating seemed to be one about not dating, but finally, I met Todd, who is a literal, not just a metaphorical, fisherman. Todd and I met at a Mexican restaurant in a town halfway between our homes. You might as well know, there is probably not a town in Texas that doesn't have a Mexican food restaurant. The small town I live in, for instance, boasts of three. I knew from a few phone conversations before the date that Todd was shy, but I had no idea just how hard the conversation would be once we met in person. While I came prepared to banter and even had a list of conversation starters in my head, I wasn't ready for every answer to be reduced to a simple word or phrase with little to no elaboration no matter how hard I dug. I shouldn't have been surprised. Think about Todd's favorite thing to do: sit in a boat for hours at a time, often alone, quietly watching a thin filament line and waiting patiently for a fish to tug on it. Another staring contest I could not win!

Before our first date, I decided to visit Bass Pro Shops to pick out a fishing lure to give Todd when we met in person. As my dating finesse evolved, I realized that something to break the ice is always a good idea. Have you ever been in the fishing section at Bass Pro Shops? There are aisles and aisles dedicated to fishing lures. I had no idea lures came in so many varieties, shapes, and colors! Apparently, everything matters: the type of water, the clarity of the water, the type of fish you're after, the size of the fish you're after, the feeding habits of the fish you're after. I think even the fish's political beliefs and sexual orientation are important based on the thousands of lures to choose from!

I was overwhelmed, so I sauntered up to the counter and politely inquired if there was anyone who really knew a lot about fishing that could give me a hand. A confident young man quickly offered to help, but I first questioned his credentials, "You've actually gone bass fishing? You catch a lot of fish when you go? When was the last time you actually caught one big enough to keep?"

I was looking for an expert because I felt like

Todd knew his stuff and would only be impressed if I brought him the Mona Lisa of lures. In my diligent search, I was surprised to learn lures often come with clever or funny names. As a matter of fact, I began to blush just a little when asking my helpful salesman if he'd had more luck with a Hula-Popper, Humpin' Toad, Eureka Wiggler, or Sweet Beaver. That question suddenly seemed to be slightly inappropriate and way too much information to share upon our first salesperson-to-customer encounter. However, he was much obliging, and I finally chose a molded, rattling, roll-resistant Whopper Plopper #75 in the color aptly called "Monkey Butt." Apparently, it was tailor-made for top-water fishing and a damn good lure; but let's be honest, after it was all said and done, I just thought the name was cute.

23
Napping with Finesse

Although Todd was a self-professed painfully shy guy, he was really clever when it came to texting. He had game as far as I could tell. For example, when I asked him what his favorite restaurant was – for the purpose of choosing an initial meeting place – his reply was, "The one where I meet you at will be my favorite." I thought that was sweet, and I enjoyed our pre-first-date flirting. We kept a running dialogue of how our respective days were going, exchanged jokes, asked questions, and sent pictures back and forth. He was endearing and complimentary. One day I told him I had run into a former student at the gym, and she had commented, "Oh, Ms. Ross, you be looking good."

He said that was a nice compliment, but I explained to him it was not a compliment at all – I had been her English teacher. The proper use of auxiliary verbs had obviously not taken hold. He laughed.

I liked that about Todd, we seemed to have a similar sense of humor. On St. Patrick's day, I came across a meme asking if it was still okay to pinch someone not wearing green or would that cause the millennials to have PTSD? Now, I don't mean any disrespect to millennials or to anyone suffering from PTSD. I am the daughter of a veteran, and my son was born in the '80s. What has happened to our collective sense of humor? If we can't laugh at ourselves and our societal shortcomings, there is no hope.

One of the things Todd and I agreed on was that

we had both failed the dating class, and neither of us was having much luck at it. I had really high hopes that once we actually met, we would click, and the funny thing is, I can't say we didn't. We met, had a nice dinner (albeit awkward conversation at times), shared a sweet goodnight kiss (okay, a series of kisses and probably a little over the top for a first date), and continued to talk. Eventually, we were able to go on a second date. Both of our dates were on weeknights because Todd spent his weekends partaking in bass tournaments on various lakes around the state of Texas. I began to see that Todd worked and fished and didn't seem to have room in his life for much else. Still, we had one final date before we stopped seeing each other.

  I met him at his house one Sunday afternoon. I was actually out of town visiting girlfriends for the weekend. Our little trio had gone to see Jason Cassidy perform at Dosey Doe in The Woodlands. Jason had been a student at one of the high schools where I taught two decades before, and I was really proud he was making a name for himself with his music career. I realized when I drove home Sunday, I could take a route that would go right through the town Todd lived in. He invited me to stop by.

  When I got there, we tried to engage in chit chat, but for all the cute and witty texting, we both seemed to clam up in person. His shyness was somehow contagious, and even I found myself at a loss for words. We were both tired, and he suggested we take a nap. I freaked out a little bit and asked, "What does that mean?" He said it just meant we should take a nap, so I hesitantly agreed.

  I think you might need a little background to understand why I'm so nervous at this point. If you remember correctly, I was married for thirty years, and I never cheated on my husband. I am a Christian woman – but not a monk or monk-ess (not a real word, but you get the idea). Up to that point, I had managed not to hop into bed with anyone (not really that hard of a task when your dating style is one and done or hanging out with a platonic friend or spending a year and a half with an inmate as your love interest), but I had grown really weary of my chaste lifestyle. Do you know how difficult it is to stick to your values when the last man you slept with was your cheating ex?

Determined to be uncorrupted, I want you to picture how seductively I approached this nap – fully clothed, I laid prostrate on the top of the bed covers and closed my eyes with the intent to sleep, similar to how someone might look while resting in a coffin. I do not know why, but Todd chose to kiss me anyway, and before I knew it, I found myself in a compromising situation, at which point I said to Todd, "My actions right now are not reflecting my values." He sighed a little and said, "Yeah, mine either."

At that point, I curled up next to him, he put his arm around my waist, and we both took a long and relaxing nap. I had not slept in a comfortable spooning position with anyone other than my husband for more than three decades. As a Christian, I knew God reserved sex for married couples. This was beyond difficult for a single woman with pent up hormones and lusty desires, but I promised myself I would at least be in a serious, committed relationship before the shaking of the sheets. It was a compromise, but I'm nothing if not transparent.

24
The Ghost in the Room

I'm not sure what Todd's final interpretation of the failed nap was, but little by little we began to ghost each other. "To ghost" is now an infinitive in the English language and "ghosting" is a noun; both reference the practice of ending a relationship with someone by disappearing from their devices. In other words, you stop calling, texting, messaging, etc. with no explanation. For us, it was gradual ghosting. Fewer texts each day for a few days and then nothing. As far as I can tell, it seemed to be mutual ghosting, so I didn't really consider it bad manners on either of our parts. In fact, we were still Facebook friends, and neither of us ever changed that status, so that puts our ending somewhere out there in limbo.

Alex had once chastised me for even considering ghosting a man I had gone out with. He said it was cowardly, and I needed to just be polite and tell the man I didn't feel like there was a connection. That's how that phrase eventually became part of the break-up template.

I might not have mentioned it, but Alex and I were simultaneously online dating. It was a symbiotic situation where I could share my experiences and get a male perspective, and vice versa, he could get the much-needed female acumen. When helping me with my profile Alex had shared a couple of women's profiles he had come across that made him just shake his head:

> *I'm a loving and good-hearted woman; however, I do not put up with men's crap. I refuse to be used, and I refuse to take care of a man! I work and expect a man to work. I'm not nobody's slave!*

Except for the two exclamation marks, I added the punctuation to that profile, which was otherwise one long run-on sentence, but I left the double negative so that you could understand her angst at the thought of being somebody's slave. Apparently, I wasn't the first woman to run into a man online whose real motive was financial gain. It is sad when women (and I suppose men as well) are reduced to looking for someone with viable employment and self-sufficiency. Another woman put it this way:

> *Looking for a fun-loving, charming intelligent man with a job and a working vehicle, US legal status, and no outstanding warrants. Must be legally divorced and single. No swingers! If you're looking for a hook-up, don't bother!* ☺

Obviously, I'm not the only one who could write a book about her failed experiences! My favorite part was the smiley face at the end. It's that type of diplomatic finesse where you tell someone to go to hell and have them looking forward to the trip. When I first began this journey, I had no idea it was necessary to expect someone to have their own mode of transportation and that you needed to stipulate it be working! However, at this point, I had pretty much caught on.

Alex had sent me a screenshot of one profile that

really shook me up. The particular site he was on afforded members the opportunity to include any other information they thought a potential suitor might want to know. This frank and nervy lady had divulged: "HSV2, a gift from my ex." Wow! I mean, I understand full disclosure, but that was putting it all out there. Let's just add one more worry to dating over fifty in this brave new world and one more reason, other than my values, not to hop from online-dating bed to online-dating bed.

    Eventually, Alex met a girl on one of those swipe left, swipe right sites where women must initiate contact, and he encouraged me to try that site. I did, but I quickly discovered there wasn't enough information for me to make a decision – there being no indication whatsoever if a man smokes or not, loves Jesus, or just wants a hook-up. Also, this site, while seemingly paying homage to my kiddie-pool side, did just the opposite. There was no way to tell whether you were swiping on a man 6'4" or 4'6" – and I was still all about the heels. Even though I had changed dating sites like most people change shoes, I bounced once again and found a third guy named David. I checked the statistics, and the decade I was born, David was the second most popular boy name, so it is not as strange as I originally thought that I kept meeting men of this moniker.

25
The Art of Indulgence

This third David knew what he wanted in a woman – almost to the point where he was aggressive about it.

> *Highly motivated and successful man seeks an equally-suited partner who is ready and willing to collaborate in life. Must be financially independent, attractive, physically and mentally fit, maintain a healthy lifestyle, intelligent, and successful in her own right. Willingness to travel and an appreciation for the finer things of life a must. No serial daters, drama or emotional instability.*

Now, with a profile like that, I would have never approached David the Third. His arrogance aside, I was not completely confident I met each and every requirement – at least not to the degree he undoubtedly expected. But he approached me. I do not know which part of my profile jumped out at him to even suggest I might be what he was looking for, but we started communicating nonetheless. From the get-go, it felt like an interview. Each question seemed like a round of "The Chase" in which I had to match wits with the Beast to determine if I would advance to the next round. Game on!

First, I was asked about my personal aspirations. Fortunately for me, I suppose, I've had a running bucket list since the divorce, and goals were no problem. For instance, I wanted to write a novel and cage-dive with Great Whites off the coast of San Francisco. I'm not sure what on that list impressed him the most, but somehow, I made it to the next round.

I am not exaggerating when I tell you that I instinctively knew a wrong answer at any point would effectively eliminate me as a dating prospect. Literally, after I sent a reply, I would get a message from David that said something very close to, "Your answer shows promise in us making a connection. I am willing to continue to spend my valuable time getting to know you." He then proceeded to ask me about my career accomplishments, how I took care of myself, whether or not I was completely healed from the divorce, and more of the same. The Facebook friend request, in hindsight, was likely another attempt to scrutinize me – and possibly even my family and friends as well. Although I had grown weary of the endless levels and examinations, we seemed to be making enough progress for a face-to-face meeting, until one of my fab-four, Darla, got involved.

Now, one thing you should know about my friend Darla is she is a spiritual giant compared to me. She has not only a close relationship with the Lord, but she keeps it consistent – not like the giant pendulum swings my spiritual life seems to take. Besides being overprotective of my well-being and virtue, she's a loveable snoop who decided I was doing such a poor job at dating that she needed to vet all future potential suitors. Further, she was also the self-proclaimed keeper of the chastity belt, a nickname John had given her when she got worried about my intentions for him when he was released. Darla is one of a kind!

And she has a knack for details. She noticed in

one of the pictures David had taken at home that there was a coffee grinder on the counter behind him. She had me ask if he ground his own coffee (because she does, and she thought that was interesting). When I asked about the grinder, I learned he didn't even drink coffee but used the grinder to grind oats in his health shakes. There are many points on which two people can be incompatible, but this one was obvious: my love of Mexican food and his quest for superiority in eating habits would never mesh.

Once again, I would have been "done" prior to ever having gone on the actual date except he broke it off as soon as I mentioned it was my friend who had noticed the coffee grinder. Apparently, he was not keen on the idea he had been the topic of two girls' discussion and scrutiny. Guys (if there are any guys actually reading this book), if a girl is not discussing you with her girlfriends, it is either because she is completely uninterested or because she has no friends. Under any other circumstances, there is no reasonable expectation you are an off-limit topic of conversation.

Also, I don't want to discourage anyone from healthy eating, but everyone should have a favorite food indulgence. Mine is the bacon sandwich. Unlike a slice of chocolate cake or a scoop of ice cream, the bacon sandwich is real sin, possibly mortal sin. Let me explain how I do a bacon sandwich. Upon deciding to indulge – and it is a willful, conscious decision to do so – I take the bacon from the fridge and arrange it in a frying pan. The sizzling, popping and crackling increase my anticipation and my mouth waters as the bacon cooks and the kitchen fills with its pungent aroma.

The smell causes me to crave, for there is no such

thing as indulgence without craving. I don't make guilt-reducing pansy sandwiches, but full-fledged, honest-to-goodness, one-hundred percent fatty, piled high with boar flesh, sandwiches; and I devour them! To even dab off the grease would lessen the experience! When I prepare the sandwich, I do not attempt to disguise the flavor or justify the calories with anything remotely wholesome. I don't reach for the lite bread; I don't cheapen the ritual by masquerading the red-and-white ribboned flesh with any tomatoes or lettuce or anything so lean and healthful. Instead, I layer and crisscross the greasy bacon onto the bread so that not one bite will be skimpier or less than the other.

Habitually, I set aside one slice of bacon for the end of my bacchanalia. Then I inhale the sandwich. I don't savor or ration – just inhale. And when I'm done and feeling just a tiny bit sad because the feast has come to a close, I remember I still have one piece left – one fried, crunchy and chewy, lard-filled piece of pig left to stimulate my nostrils, to caress my lips, to tease my tongue, and satisfy my rounded, pooching belly. There is an art to indulging that David the Third will never know, and there is a reason Darla felt a need to take on the role of the keeper of the chastity belt.

Part 4: True North

26
Cowboys and Cacti

As I'm online dating and trapesing around with Alex, I'm also checking items off the all-important bucket list. I was blessed to see the rings of Saturn and the Marfa lights on back-to-back nights in West Texas. While it was our initial plan on the West Texas trip to go to the observatory, the second adventure was an afterthought for this felicitous traveler. The day after we went to the observatory, Alex began talking about Marfa. He told me a strange phenomenon had occurred, and the town had become a mecca for the artistic crowd.

We decided to check it out for ourselves. His description was accurate; Marfa seemed to be a dichotomy – a small, dusty town with four-star restaurants, obscure galleries, elite bookstores, and historic hotels sprinkled among decaying houses, graffiti-laden dumpsters, and dilapidated storefronts. Each seemed to have a plethora of contradicting stories to tell.

We explored and photographed and partook of the offerings – a gallery with industrial minimalist sculptures that hardly seemed art if you weren't willing to stretch the imagination; a grocery store that provided a pricey gamut of gourmet, organic, and hipster foods and wares; the courtyard of a closed restaurant with a canopy of living grapes and small birds reminiscent of an Italian painting; a concept store called "Freda" filled with a hodgepodge of a locally-created patchwork of crafts.

It was in Freda that I asked the clerk – a lady who "watching the store for a friend" hardly seemed to have a vested interest in making a sale – about the Marfa lights. Since the creation of my bucket list, seeing the Marfa lights had donned the top of it. To my dismay, however, the clerk had lived there for four years and had never seen them.

While we were in the store, Alex chuckled and drew my attention to a short book he picked up and read. He told me I needed to read it, and I would know why. I took my chance and made the $14 purchase, hoping to at least support some aspiring writer, without even bothering to know the contents.

It was a gem, a delightfully told tale of fabulous friends and positivity. Alex recognized Darla, Teresa, Tammy and me immediately as the four animals in the fable. Later that night, I sent Tammy a selfie of Alex and me at the baseball game. Her response was, "You are stunning by the way." I showed her text to Alex, and we laughed at the line that was nearly lifted from the pages.

We searched for a place to eat lunch, but the finer restaurants did not open until the dining hour, so we wandered the shops of the historic Hotel Paisano and browsed the bookstore of the modern Hotel Saint George. At five, we went to be seated in the dining room of the latter and found out they were closed for even another hour.

Famished, we left and went to Jett's Grill at the Paisano. I boldly ordered ahi, which my son who has a flair for both cooking and consuming gourmet food had introduced to me the week before at Orange Beach. The medium-grilled pepper-crusted tuna with a soy, ginger, and sesame oil sauce was the absolute finest entrée I had ever eaten. Alex tasted it also and agreed it was one of the best foods he's ever tasted. The side of pistachio mashed potatoes he shared with me complemented it as well as the couscous on my plate.

We left Marfa and headed back to Alpine to watch a baseball game. As we drove past the viewing area for the Marfa lights, I got a really good daytime view of what was to the South – the Chihuahuan Desert and not much else. I didn't know it at the time, but getting a daytime view of this area would enhance the mystery I would encounter later that night.

Alex and I drove back to Alpine and searched for an evening activity. Turned out, the Alpine Cowboys of the Pecos League had a home game at Kokernot Field, a treat for both of us baseball fans. The field, as Alex explained, was historic on several accounts. Built by its namesake rancher in 1947, it is now the property of the Alpine School District, and home for both the Sul Ross State University Lobos and the headliner Cowboys.

We had driven by the field earlier that morning, and Alex had pointed out the intricately detailed baseballs in the ironworks and the native stone that came from Kokernot Ranch nestled in the nearby Davis Mountains. It smacked of authenticity, and I wasn't sure if I was more impressed by the field or Alex's knowledge of its history.

At game time we parked and both took a few pictures of the stadium as we approached. I suggested we root for the home team, and Alex shot me a look of incredulity, which reminded me I am the proud and uncontested Master of the Obvious. The crowd was light, but the people who were there seemed a dedicated bunch. Alex rummaged through the hats and t-shirts, as I pondered the symbol on the merchandise, which looked like a circle and a horseshoe lucky side up. Fitting for "Cowboys" I deduced. However, after a quick Google search, I realized I was viewing an "06," the brand of the Kokernot Ranch. Alex purchased the hat on the way out of the stadium later that night.

The game was instantly fun. A slight breeze, the shade, and green stadium chairs provided a level of unexpected comfort. The announcer alternated play-by-play with tidbits of classic rock and other fun music. The teams were fairly well matched – enough hitting and catching and stealing from both sides to keep it entertaining. Besides music that begged you to undulate and head bob, the league provided entertainment in the interludes in the form of bat girls and silly contests, such as spin around the bat for a while and race for a base.

One of the small pleasures of the game was sitting next to someone who could answer my trivial questions and fill in the gaps of my baseball rules repertoire. I was tickled when Alex donned the persona of announcer and commenced a clever monologue as a Tucson Saguaros player hit a home run: "Ramone hits it high to left field. Call the McDonald Observatory and check the trajectory. That ball was hit to the moon!"

I wish I could remember the entire diatribe, "…hometown hero for another day," but I was too caught up in enjoying it to memorize it.

Alas, the hometown heroes lost the game, 5-4, as the giant cacti took the lead in the top of the ninth. Now that is a strange mascot indeed!

27
Check It Off the Bucket List

My bucket list predates the 2008 Nicholson-Freeman hit, and most of my adult life I had wanted to see the Marfa lights. Right after the divorce, I actually wrote out my list in Notepad on my iPhone so it was always at hand, and I loyally included these phenomena. My fascination with the lights stemmed from the folk stories that surround them; the English teacher in me can't resist a good narrative or a good mystery – and they are both. The idea of the "ghost lights" brings to mind the sentiment I share with Walt Whitman:

> *When I heard the learn'd astronomer,*
> *When the proofs, the figures, were ranged in columns before me,*
> *When I was shown the charts and diagrams, to add, divide, and measure them,*
> *When I sitting heard the astronomer where he lectured with much applause in the lecture-room,*
> *How soon unaccountable I became tired and sick,*
> *Till rising and gliding out I wander'd off by myself,*
> *In the mystical moist night-air, and from time to time,*
> *Look'd up in perfect silence at the stars.*

Science spoils mystery. On occasion, I prefer the illogical and inexplicable to the plausibly explained. Point in case, the Marfa lights and the perfect silent stars I was about to witness.

Because we spent the afternoon and early evening in Marfa and driving back to Alpine for the baseball game, I did not expect we would return to the area on this trip; but to my pleasant surprise, Alex suggested it at the conclusion of the baseball game. So we drove west on Hwy. 67, and I struggled to reign in my expectations. The lady at Freda's, after all, said she had lived in Marfa for four years and had not been able to see the lights. Alex told me some people live in Marfa their entire lives and do not see them. Earlier that day, I tried to hedge my bets by nailing down a specific time during the night the lights might show up or a specific weather pattern for optimal viewing – anything. For my efforts, I was assured it's basically a crap shoot.

Riding in the passenger seat, I made an attempt to quell my hopes; I considered the odds that the lights would appear on this random night, at this arbitrary time when we would show up to gaze at the sky in unrealistic expectation. But I was reminded in my spirit that my heavenly father gave me Saturn on a cloudy night, and I prayed, "Father, could I also see the Marfa lights?"

It seemed a short drive to reach the viewing area – a rest-stop type structure sans the "well-lit" one would expect. Instead, as at the observatory, red lighting close to the ground marked the walking path to a stone wall that is the outer most edge of the viewing facility. As we walked to view, a few others were leaving, and I eavesdropped on their conversations to try to ascertain if there had been any mysterious sightings. To my disappointment, it seemed a dull evening so far.

For a moment we stood at the wall and just gazed at the heavens. Unlike the night before, this sky was crystalline. For the first time in my life, I understood what it meant to be in the midst of the

Milky Way. The galaxy belt in my view was no longer abstract and separate, but immense – almost reachable – and Earth's position in the midst of it evident. So many more stars were visible than what I'm used to partaking that the constellations were hidden by the very things that make them up. Alex and I each quickly spotted separate shooting stars, and I had the familiar thought, "If I see nothing else, this is magnificent." I decided I must climb over the bar railing and sit on the stone wall for full effect. Alex was a little concerned I wasn't aware of how far down the drop on the other side of the wall was, but I didn't plan to fall, and – more importantly – I trusted him not to let me. I simply reminded him my kids expected him to bring me home safely.

In spite of my satisfaction with the brilliance of the stars, God – in amusement or delight – had a better show in mind. After just a few minutes, a light appeared in the sky. I quickly turned to Alex, "Did you see that?" He grinned and said he did. And a few minutes later, another one. Then two together. Then one zigzags in an inexplicable way. It was like watching giant fireflies – intermittent and flashing, erratic in space, appearing and disappearing.

I literally could not contain my excitement, and I reached and grabbed Alex's hand that was resting on the railing and held on to it. I simply could not experience this without connecting to another human and having the assurance we were synchronized – our senses and our responses in tandem. And although I didn't want to distract anyone around me, jubilation was bubbling from my core, and I was absolutely giddy. I turned to gauge Alex's expression and had the distinct feeling he was propitiating me with yet another first as he was prone to do. After all, he had seen the lights before.

As we watched the apparitions – for what would prove to be over an hour – a man came and sat on the wall just a little way down from me. He began a tribal-type chant that, for me, set a perfect mood. His voice was transcendent, and the rhythm of the chant escorted me to a different time and place – an anthropological primal setting. I whispered to Alex, "I know you're probably weirded out by his chanting, but I think it's beautiful."

And with heightened senses, I was also counting shooting stars. At the fifth one, I thought, "Make a wish." My immediate response to my own imperative was "I have nothing to wish for." And I didn't. At that moment, I couldn't have been in a better place, with better company, or with a better view.

In all, I counted ten shooting stars that night in Marfa. In one moment, I saw five of the mysterious lights at once lined up across the horizon. So silently but with exuberance, I thanked my God for inexplicably gifting me the rings of Saturn and the Marfa lights back to back and for the guide beside me who first imagined these destinations and accompanied me on this journey.

28
Sabbatical at Miramar

When my daughter turned thirteen, I encouraged her to have her own bucket list, which she was predisposed to do anyway. Her list is unique from mine, but there are a few crossovers. One thing neither of us had yet done but both desired to do was parasail. I got to check it off during my fifty-third summer of life. Darla invited five of her girlfriends to stay in a condo with her at Miramar Beach. It was an eclectic group – some of which were meeting for the first time. What we had in common was we each knew Darla in some walk of life. For me, Darla is the closest of my fab four; Jill is another one of my best friends and was my running buddy when we taught English together; Susan is a dear friend and was the counselor at the high school when I was the principal; Sue is from the same town and an acquaintance I was excited to get to know better; and I was meeting Linda, Jill's sister-in-law, for the first time.

Susan and I drove up together, turning a twelve-hour trip into about fourteen. As the navigator, my distractions and diversions took us on a few detours before finally arriving at the condo that can only be described as magnificent. It was directly on the beach, and our unit on the third floor was one of only eight facing the ocean. Every morning we awoke to breathtaking views from our seventy-foot long balcony, and every evening, drinks in hand, we imbibed in God-inspired sunsets, starry skies, full moon, and even a summer storm.

Of my friends who shared in the Epicurean sea and sand adventure with me, it was Jill who suggested I read one of her recent favorite novels because she believed I led a life very similar to the author who had written it. So I bought the book in a quaint little used bookstore on 30A in Watercolor, Florida, and read it under an umbrella on the beach between long swims in the ocean.

Two things had happened a week before I left for this trip. John and I had reconnected and agreed to try to be friends, and I had exchanged phone numbers with a new online match. So as I imbibed in the beach wonderland, I was also intermittently texting and talking to Mark. Getting to know him would coincide with falling in love with the ocean.

I had been to many beaches throughout my life, mostly while chasing my children or grandchildren, Emery and Jase. I found them to be fun but also sandy and hot and sticky and tiring – the beaches, not the grandkids. Okay, maybe the grandkids just a little. This was my first time on a beach in at least three decades without any little ones that I had to make sure didn't wander off or go too deep or wipe the sand out of their eyes or something similar that distracted me from really taking in the splendor of God's great ocean and all that it encompasses.

My very first morning on the beach I had an epiphany – I could close my eyes. Seriously, I could close my eyes for as long as I wanted without worry or neglect to some sort of duty, and I could let my other senses take over. As I listened to the crashing waves, smelled the salty air, and felt the warming sun, I let go of anxiety and stress in a way I hadn't done in a long time. Without realizing it, my relationship with the beach transformed, and I fell in love. I pondered whether or not we do that with people at times but in reverse. We fall in love initially but then we get caught up trudging through the sand, becoming hot and sticky and tired, worrying the waves crashing over us will drown us; or at the very least, we're busy wiping the stinging sweat from our eyes until we don't remember what it was like to love at all. On Miramar Beach, somehow, my life simplified and unclogged, and I felt only alive and blessed and in the moment.

The book I was reading that week on the beach resonated with my profound heartbreak in losing John and with a recent dating debacle – Scotty. Although I was already talking to someone new, I needed the salty waters of the Gulf of Mexico to wash over me and heal a broken spirit and put my emotions back into perspective. About three months prior to this trip I met a man online who would finally be my stereotypical rebound relationship and self-inflicted fall from grace.
Instead of rebounding as most would after a failed thirty-year marriage, it was the hurt from Leavenworth I rebelled against. And in the true sense of rebound, I disregarded my conscience and my beliefs to mute the leftover pain and loneliness and found myself uncharacteristically carrying on a brief but passionate affair with Scotty, a man I barely knew and I didn't love.

The night I met him, my kiddie pool took over, he was handsome and muscle-bound and nearly a decade my junior – and something about him reminded me of John. My thin-slicing was screaming this was a mismatch from the beginning. We didn't share anything in common – beliefs, values, experiences, or goals – but my internal disaster warning system was effectively shut down with the first kiss, and I managed to completely ignore the alarm bells that were going off, begging for me to recognize the inconsistencies and bullshit. I fell fully, deeply, and rapidly in lust with a man who fulfilled my shallowest of desires and avenged my broken heart. On the second date, we worked out. I was sans make-up, hot, and sweaty, and he bent down and kissed me and said, "I'm going to marry you someday." In that moment, I allowed myself to believe him. What he meant to say – what would have been truthful – was, "I'm still married, but I'm hoping you and I can hook up anyway." By the way, ladies, if you can't go to his house or even his home town, if his phone is always on silent and face down, and if he constantly breaks plans suddenly and with lame excuses, he might be married.

I had belied my true nature, which is to be very selective and reserve intimacy for a meaningful relationship. I broke off the affair upon discovering I had been lied to and resolved to return to true north, to not continue to engage the primal urges Scotty had satisfied and stirred. It felt painful and restrictive. When I first arrived in Miramar, I was still wrestling with my own concoction of fond memories, invigorated senses, guilt, and condemnation.

When I was a young girl, I was obsessed with the dandelion. These weeds we mistakenly call flowers come in two phases – as simple yellow blooms that signal the onset of spring and as feather-like white balls that signal the beginning of summer. That's the phase when I like dandelions the most. To the disdain of gardeners everywhere, I still stop and pick one every now and then just to blow the fluff into the air and make a wish like I did when I was a kid. Of course, that's how they replenish and spread. What I didn't know until I was an adult was dandelions symbolized both emotional healing and the power of the sun. I get that – the blowing away of the old to create something new and the rejuvenation we feel when the sun breaks through winter gray with its healing rays.

At this particular juncture more than others, I needed the clarity of sun and salt water. Laying on that beach in Miramar, God's breath and forgiveness came as an ocean breeze that blew away the fuzzy excess and unclogged the pores of the past four years. I was truly ready to just be myself again, even if – especially if – that meant being by myself.

After several lazy days on the beach watching parasailers in the distance, I knew it was time to cross that off of my bucket list. I asked my companions to join me. One had never parasailed and assured me her status was not changing on this trip. A couple of them had parasailed in the '70s and remembered having to run down the beach to catch enough wind to be lifted off the ground. They were not really interested in revisiting the activity.

It was Linda who was adventurous enough to agree to go with me. We found an outfitter and made a reservation. It was an absolutely incredible experience. The captain of the boat – a hunky, bare-chested, twenty-something-year-old boy – boasted of sending his thrill seekers eight-hundred feet into the air. I don't know if we were actually that high, but I do know sailing above the gulf over the dark blue choppy waters teaming with life and death was one of the most calming and peaceful places I had ever been.

My friend of a little less than a week was much

more nervous than I was. In fact, surprisingly, I wasn't nervous at all. Anyway, when we landed back on the deck of the boat, she kissed my cheek and said, "I love you." I think she was grateful to have survived. At that moment, Linda and I became friends for life.

Parasailing and making a life-long friend in the process brought me to the conclusion life is absolutely about love. This is totally congruent with my faith and trust in God and Jesus who loved us enough to give His life. But it is a relatively new thing for how I feel about myself. I've always held myself in condemnation – guilty as charged of original sin and all others. It's quite ironic that after my recent dive into fornication, which was really adultery unbeknownst to me, I had finally come to love and accept myself. Several nights later at Miramar, there was a fantastic summer storm. As soon as the rain and lightning subsided, Linda and I waded out into the ocean about knee deep against the advice of the maternal friend, Darla, who is always trying to save me from myself (and who is obsessed to the point of paranoia about sharks feeding nocturnally) to look for sand dollars and other sea creatures. I was compelled to do it – the storm chilled the air more than the water – the antithesis of what you normally experience at the beach. I am all about perspective. This act brought me full circle to evaluate my life and dating since the divorce. To my own surprise and delight, in that evaluation there was no broken heart or longing for any past relationship, not even for John. There was no condemnation or lust, not even for Scotty. There was no angst at the thought of my numerous failed dating encounters. There were just memories of these things – and they weren't all bad.

Ultimately on that trip, I swam in the ocean over

my head in broad daylight – literally in the blue-green waters of Miramar Beach – and figuratively in the dating scene in which I had become ensconced over the past four years. Both could have been a little dangerous given the right circumstances, but it turned out that up to this point I had survived the two – swimming and dating – with little thought to what could have been lurking beneath while I was daring and exposed. This galvanized perspective gave me the confidence to continue dating or to be alone and not date at all. So talking with Mark was without pressure. I didn't feel a need to date – and didn't even know if I wanted to. Further, I had sifted through my heart and mind and decided I was grateful for every experience, including what I had with John. I accepted the totality of it without any regret. I embraced the idea of daring and exposed...and I committed to pursuing it more.

29
Not Preacher Wife Material

Thus, the time at the beach demarcated a turning point in my life – the second one since the divorce. Unlike losing John, this one was more of perspective than circumstances, but it changed how I approached online dating. Mark was probably the coolest of all my online connections. Of course, it probably helped that our first conversations were in the backdrop of Miramar sunsets. Most of my friends in the condo were early risers who went to bed early. I'm a night owl, and so is Mark. After everyone else retired for the evening, I would sit on the balcony and talk to him. Like me, he is an outdoor enthusiast and has a great appreciation for God's creation. He hung out on the beach vicariously that week; I shared pictures of myself, the water, sunsets, food – just about everything I imbibed in.

One night, my musings of wondering if Mark just might be Saturn came to a screeching halt. I had overlooked asking him about his profession, which is usually one of the first things you talk about when you meet someone online. However, upon learning what he did for a living, I knew why he, at least, had avoided the topic. He has one of those jobs that scares the heebie-jeebies out of women and causes them to run full force in the opposite direction: Mark is a Methodist preacher. Now, I have the utmost respect for the clergy, but I am about the farthest thing on the planet from preacher-wife material. That was my exact reaction to Mark's confession of profession, "Mark, I am so sorry, but I am NOT preacher wife material."

He laughed as if he'd heard it many times before or as if it weren't really true, so I had to explain to him I wasn't kidding. I told him that, although out of character, I had been intimate with the last guy I dated. In fact, when it came to the Ten Commandments, I was pretty sure I had now broken just about all of them, with the possible exception of murder; and even at that, I had killed a donkey once.

About the donkey, I was a city girl – or at least a suburbs girl – moving to the country, and the first thing I wanted to experience in this new town was the auction barn. Growing up, my grandmother had run an auction barn café, and my brothers and I used to scurry around the catwalks watching cowboys prod the cattle through. Auction barns had always fascinated me. So one afternoon, I went up there to watch the cattle sale. Well, they ran a donkey out first, and no one seemed interested. I asked a rancher, "What happens if no one buys it?"

"Glue factory," was his uninterested reply.

I was mortified and decided to save the donkey by bringing it home with me. If you know anything about donkeys, you probably already know this was a stupid idea. By the way, at that time I didn't even own a trailer to haul the donkey back to my house. In my impetuousness, I guess I thought I could buckle the donkey in the backseat.

Well, $35.00 later and with the goodwill of a rancher who lived near me, I got the donkey to my house and tied it to a tree because I didn't have a corral to put it in. I had no idea donkeys don't wait patiently when tied up. I have seen quite a few Westerns where the cowboy merely has to wrap his horse's reins loosely around a pole as he enters the saloon, and the horse will wait in that exact spot for however long it takes the cowboy to get wet his whistle, shoot the bad guy, and kiss the girl. I thought donkeys and horses were like first cousins and could be treated just about the same. I have since learned that is not the case. This donkey, in particular, did not like being tied to the tree one bit and started wrapping itself around and around until there was no rope left. I don't want to go into the gory details, but the donkey basically hung himself on that tree with that rope. When I discovered him, it was a gruesome sight, and I was beyond upset. I called my dad to come and help me, and his exact words of comfort were, "Egads! Keri, that animal suffered." In hindsight, the donkey might have preferred the glue factory.

Mark's reply to my confession of breaking all ten commandments, including murdering a donkey was, "Well, donkeys are overrated." Now, I'm not Methodist, and I only know two Methodist preachers, but they both have a great sense of humor and are the most genuine people I have ever met. It almost makes me want to convert, but it's not enough to entertain the idea of rendering the sacrifices necessary to be married to a man of the cloth.

However, Mark and I went on to meet and become friends, and his friendship helped to reconcile my spiritual incongruences. He has a refreshing perspective when it comes to God that guided me past my condemnation and my upbringing, which was something akin to the Puritan's "Sinners in the Hands of an Angry God." He's one of those preachers who isn't religious; he just genuinely loves people and God, and he was able to help me refocus and be reminded I'll never be good enough for God – and thankfully, I don't have to be. He loves me anyway. My latest bout of online dating seemed to at least be producing friendships. And I think Mark would probably agree with me that if you have the opportunity and the right relationship, you should make love every day – more than once if possible – suck the marrow! And you should pray every day – more than once if possible – and you should know those two things are more alike than different.

30
Sei pronto per una grande avventura?

My time at Miramar had been so impactful that I wanted to take my daughter there as soon as possible; after all, parasailing was on her bucket list as well. My friend Susan must have felt the same way because she found out the condo we were staying at had a cancellation the following month, and she booked it. I'm just going to be honest here – I invited myself and my daughter to join Susan and her daughter.

As bad as that sounds, Susan is a really good friend and would have just told me no if she didn't like the idea; however, true to her laid back and accommodating nature, she welcomed us. Conversely, looking back, if Susan has a passive-aggressive side, she did get us both hooked on vanilla Frappuccino, which by the bottle is high in both calories and cost if you consume one every single day, sometimes multiple bottles a day!

The following month, I was packed and headed to the beach again. This time with my daughter, we adopted a theme for our trip: *Sei pronto per una grande avventura?* That's Italian for, "Are you ready for a great adventure?" We had decided to learn a little Italian – at least enough to order a steak and ask, "Where is the bathroom?" – because we intend to go to Italy after Jilly's college graduation, a newer addition to the bucket list.

After my initial week on the beach my mindset returned to what I already knew – the lesson I had taken away from rock climbing years ago – it's not about the destination but the journey, and each and every day is a great adventure in all ways – physically, spiritually, emotionally. I couldn't wait to share this perspective and a beautiful locale with my lovely sidekick.

Like Alex, she is also a wonderful traveling companion. We like the same music, don't mind detours or unplanned stops, appreciate the scenery, and engage in delightful conversation.

When I had first started dating, I explained to Jilly why I was ready to venture out and meet men. I laid some ground rules for myself, including I wouldn't introduce anyone I was dating to her, and I wouldn't date on the weekends when she was with me. She would remain my priority. I wanted a balance of keeping her insulated but also keeping her in the loop and being honest with her. We had both had to deal with our fair share of lies that messed up our lives, so honesty was paramount.

I also wanted her to have a little bit of a voice in this situation because her life had been impacted so dramatically by the divorce, and she had been thrust into a situation where she had little to no control. So before I ever went on the first date, I invited her to make a list of what she might want to see in a stepdad, if it ever came to that.

Her list included some things that were not at all surprising – a man who believed in God, loved animals, and treated her mother well – but it also included a thing or two that made me wonder and chuckle. For instance, the man must love Pop Tarts, specifically one of three flavors – raspberry, brown sugar cinnamon, or cookies 'n cream. That was odd because while I might be a kiddie pool, my daughter's well runs deep. I knew she loved Pop Tarts, but I had no idea why a new stepdad must also. When I dug deeper, the answer was one of those things that kicked me in the gut.

The day my divorce became final and I stood before a judge to announce to the world my ex and I had failed in our thirty-year marriage, I stood there alone. He did not bother to show up for this formality. Instead, unbeknownst to me, he was moving the girlfriend into what used to be our home. That very day.

As it turned out, the girlfriend liked strawberry Pop Tarts, which my daughter wasn't fond of. On that day, my ex stopped buying the flavors my daughter liked and only bought strawberry Pop Tarts. For her, that act was indicative of how her life had changed overall; and in a new step dad, she was hoping for someone who would value her choices and selflessly pick out something with her in mind, like raspberry Pop Tarts.

My list was simple – I was basically looking for a Christian version of Keanu Reeves. (Not saying Keanu Reeves isn't a Christian – I just have no idea of his belief system, and I know what is important to me. To Keanu's credit, I have read he is one of the most unassuming and humble men around in spite of his superstar status. I just know he's dashingly handsome and well built, and he has kind and penetrating eyes that seem to look into the soul of whoever is lucky enough to be on the other end of that stare. If anything, I would love to find an unpretentious man with eyes like that – and muscles. Never forget muscles.)

Speaking of muscles, I booked the same charter

for our parasailing adventure, remembering the young, tanned deckhand of the previous trip. I wondered if my daughter would be nervous or daring as we lifted off the boat and rapidly ascended to eight-hundred feet, and my answer came quickly. She was thrilled and mesmerized by the view and the adventure. We tried to make out objects in the water beneath us – mostly trying to distinguish between large fish swimming close to the surface or shadows cast by the fluffy clouds on that bright-blue day. We wondered at the vastness of the gulf, remarking that this was only the gateway to an even more expansive ocean. We marveled how God separated land and sea and somehow set a boundary between them.

We had spent the day before we parasailed lazily on the beach. The conditions were ideal; the water even calmer and bluer than it had been the month before. A bloom of sand-dollar-sized jellyfish had come into the area we were swimming, and we learned the smaller jellyfish didn't sting, so we caught them in our hands to marvel at their structure.

We sighted a stingray swimming past, and eventually, a small shark swam near us and the other beachgoers. True to our theme of having a great adventure, we chased the shark up and down the beach with curiosity and novel engagement. We were in the moment – and the destination didn't matter at all.

As we traveled home, we had great conversation. As we were talking about overcoming fears, the topic inevitably turned to my daughter's phobia: bees. For a girl who is daring enough to chase a shark up and down a beach, it might be surprising to learn she's petrified of these small flying, albeit stinging, insects.

I told her about an episode of NOVA I had seen that was centered on the Gurung tribe of Nepal, which is located in a beautiful jungle. The Gurung people, twice a year, trek out into the scenic countryside to locate the hives of the Himalayan honeybee, and in aboriginal form, collect its golden wealth.

The hives are always located under the overhang of precarious cliffs, and the Gurung have to belay over the precipice on hand-made rope ladders to get to them. They are not in any other way tethered and trust these rickety ladders and their fellow tribesmen who are securing them from above with their very lives.

As they climb down the ladders and reach the hives, they are in the midst of tens of thousands of honeybees determined to guard their home and labor. Sans protective bee suits, the men on the ladders use primitive barbs attached to ropes and guided by a pole to stabilize the hive so that when it's cut, it won't plummet to the ground only to have its contents explode on impact, but instead can be gently lowered. The cutting tool is also on a long pole furthering the need for good balance but affording a little distance from the hive's defenders. Each hive filled with honey weighs about fifty pounds, and on a successful mission, the Gurung will return to the village with hundreds of pounds of waxy treasure.

In spite of the cinematography and characterization of the Gurung people, my favorite part of the story was a footnote that had to do with the hive itself. Scientists have done in-depth studies of why the compartments of a hive are hexagonal when any shape with tessellation properties would work. Why not a square or a triangle?

The answer is because the hexagon is the perfect

shape for the task – it allows for maximum surface area and holding capacity for the honey while allowing the worker bee to put forth the least amount of energy in constructing it. The scheme is optimal, and scientists cannot come up with a better way to design a hive in spite of their computer-generated models and advanced degrees! For me, the more I study math and science, the more it proves God and never disproves him. I have always been intrigued by the Fibonacci spiral – the mathematical laws and the patterns that show up in nature: the sunflower, the pine cone, a seashell. The golden ratio, pi, base ten – I could never believe the universe was accidental and not by design of an omniscient, omnipresent, omnipotent God; although, admittedly, I don't always understand why things happen the way they do.

I thought this was a brilliant mom-moment, espousing to my daughter the value of bees and the divine design of their earthly endeavors and relating their contributions to God's greater design of pattern and order.

Her reply brought me back to reality, "Mom, it's not really bees I'm afraid of so much as wasps." I had no insight on wasps and unfortunately could not immediately champion the small creature or espouse its virtues or contributions to the greater good with the possible exception that I knew of at least one species made a habit of killing spiders. There's always a silver lining.

Did I even mention that at least one of my good friends often referred to me as Pollyanna? (Actually, she referred to me as "Bitchy-Anna." I never knew exactly what that meant beyond it being some sort of mismatched hybrid of being optimistically difficult?)

Part 5: Destination Deferred

31
Give That Man Some Licorice

When I returned the second time from Miramar, I resumed my online quest, and I started talking to a gentleman named Wayne. He didn't live that far away, and he knew a few people in my hometown. We didn't have any of the same friends, but it was way closer than seven degrees of Kevin Bacon. In fact, I think it was three, and that little bit of proximity caused me to once again let my guard down. In fact, I broke several of my cardinal rules. For instance, never let an online date pick you up at your house. Set a time limit of fewer than two hours for the initial date. And, finally, the first meeting should be a simple lunch or dinner. If you hit it off, you can always plan another date. If you don't, you need a time limit – and an exit. Allowing a date to pick you up at your house not only compromises your safety, but it also allows for extra awkwardness on the ride home if the date doesn't go well.

Against my better judgment, I had agreed to allow Wayne to pick me up from my house since he was familiar with the town; and worse, he had asked if we could meet earlier than originally planned, get lunch, see a movie, and hang out that evening as well. Online dating rules are not made to be broken!

It was upon meeting Wayne I learned a picture may be worth a thousand words, but those words can be very misleading. While it was obvious the man standing at my front door was technically the same man in the pictures I had seen, he did not at all look the same. His hair was styled differently, and by that I mean, it wasn't washed or styled at all and hung down in his eyes. His clothes were wrinkled and had a pungent mildew smell, and he hung his shoulders and shuffled when he walked. None of this had been conveyed in any of the images I had seen. The man had a nice face, but I found his overall presentation to be a complete turnoff.

Once again, I became acutely aware of my kiddie-pool self. In my defense, however, there have actually been studies done on attractiveness, and it has been discovered auditory and olfactory cues are just as important as visual cues. In fact, vanilla, black licorice, and cinnamon have been identified as three odors that are not only pleasant but engage our senses and impact sexual arousal. Mildew, by the way, did not even make the top ten!

I figured the mildew smell was indicative of a recently divorced man who probably wasn't used to doing his own laundry. Again, if there are any men reading this book who are new to this chore, never leave wet clothes in the washing machine for any length of time. As soon as the cycle ends, transfer the clothes to the dryer (preferably with a licorice-scented dryer sheet) and turn it on! And if you're not keen on ironing, as soon as the dryer gets near the end of the cycle, make sure the clothes are completely dry, and take them out and hang them up. In the back of my mind, I kept thinking if Wayne and I by some miracle hit it off on another level, then I could easily correct the mildew snafu. Don't forget – Pollyanna.

There are two movie theaters relatively close to my house. One is forty-five minutes away; the other is an hour and fifteen minutes away. When you live in a small town in Texas, driving an hour for a movie is not all that uncommon. Remembering I had committed to hanging out with this guy for an entire afternoon and evening, I chose to go to the theater that was the furthest away. I needed to kill some time, and I had the least chance of running into someone I knew. If I'm being honest, Wayne looked a little like he lived on the streets, and I'm sure at this point there were those people around town who assumed my dating life was such a disaster that I was just desperate enough to pick up someone on a street corner holding a sign "will date for food."

I was not proud of the myriad of thoughts like these that were running through my head. I try to be empathetic and helpful towards people who are less fortunate and deal with difficult circumstances, such as homelessness...always remembering, "But by the grace of God, there goes me."

We decided on a sports bar for lunch where I knew the food would be delicious. The conversation during the ride to the restaurant had been awkward and filled with long pauses when no one said anything. I hoped sitting across from my date would facilitate talking and one or both of us would be able to pick up the pace and come up with some interesting banter. Upon meeting our waitress, I initially thought this might come to fruition – she had an identical tattoo to the man sitting across from me, and it seemed to be a great conversation starter. Since John, I am a fan of a quality tattoo strategically located. I would like to claim it's because of a lingering rebellion from a fairly strict upbringing or a side effect of my love for aesthetically pleasing art; but the truth of the matter is, it's because of the hours I sat in the USDB, holding John's hands and tracing with my fingers the tattoos on his forearms. The fact Wayne had an interesting tattoo was actually a plus for him, and it was a bit of a coincidence for the waitress to share it. In hindsight, I should have tried to hook them up.

Besides the tattoo, we could find little to talk about and really began to discover we were opposites in most things. We didn't have similar religious, political, or financial views – those little things that hardly matter! So instead of picking up steam, the conversation did the opposite. The longer we sat and got to know each other, the less we had to say, and the more we felt like strangers. There were long, awkward periods of silence, which Wayne occasionally tried to break by asking, "What are you thinking?"

Truth be told, I was thinking, "You don't want to know what I'm thinking." Because all I could think about was how did I get in this situation, and how could I get out? Where did I take a wrong turn in this online dating process to end up sitting across from a man I didn't find attractive, I didn't find intellectually stimulating, and I didn't find his personality appealing? How could someone be so different online versus in the flesh? These were the questions that were bombarding my brain and blocking it from retrieving any other fodder for conversation, so I replied stupidly, "I dunno."

I am fully aware there are two sides to every story. I have to admit if some of the guys I went out with were the ones telling the story instead of me, there is a really good chance I did not make a great impression. I'm sure each could complain.

Crazy Curtis might have said he went out with

this girl with no sense of adventure. David the First could lament he went out with a girl who didn't know how to have fun (or undress). Todd the Fisherman could certainly make fun of my nap-taking prowess. And Wayne would be correct in surmising – at least for our date – that I was a poor conversationalist who couldn't come up with a single fresh idea.

Mercifully, lunch ended, and we decided on a movie. As we walked to the theater, Wayne moved closer to me and put his arm around me, completely ignoring my uncomfortableness and the lack of connection we had established for the past hour – or rather failed to establish. As we approached the theater, to my horror, I ran into that one fake-friendly woman in town that spreads gossip as easily as butter on hot toast. There was nothing I could do but make eye-contact and exchange a greeting. In every sense of the word, I felt exposed.

Unfortunately, Wayne had to drive me home, and he had left his jacket in my house that afternoon when he picked me up. That meant I actually had to allow him to come inside to retrieve it. The awkward chit-chatting droned on in the living room, and he leaned in to kiss me. I quickly turned my head so that he got a lip full of cheek. The date ended with me spouting the break-up template in person when poor Wayne seemed oblivious to the nonverbal cues I had been sending since the onset, bless his heart. (This is just an aside, but you do know it is acceptable for a Southern woman to say anything she likes about someone no matter how mean it is if she prefaces it with "bless his heart"?)

Once again, I would like to address any males who might be reading this. Please watch the movie

Hitch. There is a notable scene where the Date Doctor teaches his hapless client about the good night kiss. You never go the whole way! Lean in ninety percent, and if she's interested, she will meet you the rest of the way. Men with game know and practice this! John was in prison, and he knew this! (By the way, if she doesn't meet you that other ten percent, chances are she sent tons of nonverbal cues prior to that to let you know not to even make an attempt. Bless your heart!)

It was late when Wayne left, but I had to talk to someone to process this disaster date, and Alex was the obvious choice. I was a bit frazzled and told him I was failing miserably at online dating and I felt too old for this nonsense. I think he was taken aback at my uncharacteristically pessimistic attitude when I bemoaned, "I just can't do this."

He simply said, "You thought you couldn't draw either."

32
Dining with Stravinsky, Picasso, and Einstein

He was right. I was one of those people who fully understood I could not draw. For my entire five decades, even my stick figures were substandard and barely recognizable as the images they represented. I believed drawing was an innate talent – one I obviously did not possess.

It was right after I moved out and was trying to furnish and decorate my new house after the divorce that I asked Alex, who had a knack for drawing, to do a sketch for me to frame and mount on the wall. He told me to do one myself, but I assured him I couldn't draw. Have I mentioned how hard it is to win an argument with Alex?

He told me, "Yes, you can. You're just using the wrong side of your brain." And unbeknownst to me, he set out to prove it.

Stravinsky, Picasso, and Einstein – never have three men exemplified the whole of the brain more than these. A composer, an artist, a physicist – what better triad to merge the intellect and the creative? The vertices of their existence intrigue me, their mutual effort to draw on classical precedent for inspiration only to add chaos and controversy and eventually genius to the canon of their respective fields.

So almost four years prior to my date with Wayne, when Alex met me for what was supposed to be a simple lunch date, these three figures intersected at a corner table in a restaurant we occupied. Alex was determined I learn this lesson, and he showed up with pencils, drawing paper, and a hardback copy of *Drawing on the Right Side of the Brain*, which included Picasso's drawing of Stravinsky.

Alex intended to prove me wrong and show me I could indeed draw. He started instructing. My first exercise was to draw some lines, but he coached me how to look at the lines from a different perspective, to tinker with my mind and close one portal and open another. He told me to focus on what I really saw using the right side of my brain and not what I thought I saw – the symbols the left side tried to conjure.

I engaged in the metacognition of the raging war in my intellect, and I was humored by how clear the battle suddenly became. It was as if I felt the firing synapses when I favored one side of the brain to the other, and I navigated a minefield of purposeful and random thoughts to focus on seeing what was really there – white spaces, smudges, shadings – instead of the objects my left brain attempted to substitute.

As I did this, my first drawing was a topsy-turvy attempt that lent to a surprising outcome. The man across from me was correct: anyone can draw. In spite of the intimidation, of not wanting to fail as the teacher watched, I began to see what was really there.

He turned the picture I was emulating upside down so that I didn't see a man in a chair. I saw a line, a longer line, a curve, a circle, a smudge of black. It became easier until I lost focus briefly and saw a knee, a finger, two hands that didn't quite connect. As I struggled to draw, Alex reminded me of the task. He remained patient and encouraging.

And eventually, he withdrew and began to work

himself, and Einstein entered the arena. The theoretical physicist whose work was both genius and catastrophic. I momentarily drifted and thought about the Manhattan Project, but that became a distraction – and he noticed and commented about being able to see the struggle between my right and left-brain. I didn't reveal how far off task I had gotten at that moment and returned to the primary objective – drawing Stravinsky.

I continued to glance occasionally at the emerging scientist on Alex's sketch pad and was increasingly impressed and daunted. The task before me blurred, and I reached for the eraser in his hand. In tandem and silence, he passed it. The synchronization quietly astonished me, and I was equally astonished when I turned my own drawing around and observed an image actually similar to the original. Unbelievably, with one single lesson and in only one attempt, I had overcome my stick-figure bests and just drawn Igor Stravinsky, almost identically to Pablo Picasso's 1920 portrait, with the exception of skewed hands – the point at which I lost focus.

I assured myself this was a fluke, and the next night, alone in my home, I attempted the exercise again. This time I drew a hand. I started with the pinky, and as soon as it was completed, I wanted to quit because, to my amazement, it actually looked like a little finger. I pressed on until the hand was almost completed but lost confidence and stopped abruptly.

To make a long story short, I've attempted to draw five or six times now – some attempts more successful than others. If I tap into this certain spot in my right hemisphere, this spot that I can almost feel when I access it, I can do it. And every time I do, it is an amazing and crazy experience that reinforces the mindset of never being too old or too inept to learn, to change, to create, to do.

33
Mom and the Surfer Dude

I had yet another epiphany about my online dating: I was seeing what I thought was there – not what really was. There is an old joke that says, "A woman marries a man thinking he will change; a man marries a woman thinking she won't." Obviously, both end up disappointed in that scenario. As I was reading the information provided online, I think I was applying my own template of what I thought was there – what I hoped to find in a man – not what was actually there. And worse, even when I saw some things that weren't a good match, I thought they might be fixable. The bottom line, I was not meshing well with my dates in many cases simply because I was not vetting well from the moment I read the online profile.

Perception is always something that has fascinated me. I remembered one night my son called me and asked if I still had those books about that bear family I had read to him as a child, deliberately not pronouncing *Berenstain*.

I said, "Do you mean the *Berenstein Bears*?"

"Yes, Mom." He replied. "How do you spell *Berenstein*?"

This one was easy for me, I had always pronounced the title *bear-in-stine*, and I knew that *e* before *i* makes the long *i* sound, where *i* before *e* makes the long *e* sound. So I spelled, "*b-e-r-e-s-t-e-i-n*."

He said, "No, mom, that's not correct."

I said, "Really? Because I'm pretty sure the *e*

comes before the *i*, but maybe it's *i-e*."

He said, "No, it's spelled with an *a*."

I swore to him I had read those books dozens of times, and if it had been spelled with an *a*, then I would have pronounced the name *bear-in-stane*, which I most definitely did not do. I was so sure I was right, I jumped on my computer to prove to him just that. Of course, that is when I learned the *Berenstain Bear* books were victim of the Mandela Effect.

The Mandela Effect is a used to describe the phenomena of a large number of people remembering something falsely or having a clear memory of something that never happened. It gets its name from the South African civil rights activist Nelson Mandela. When Mandela died in 2013, many adults were confused because they swore they remembered him dying in prison in the '80s. There's actually a more scientific term for collective memory errors – *confabulation*.

From my drawing experience, I knew the brain could replace what you actually see with symbols; from thin-slicing, I knew the brain created templates to give you gut feelings; and from my research on the Mandela Effect (because that was just too cool to ignore), I knew the brain could provide you with inaccurate memories (or evidence you've experience an alternate reality, depending on whose perspective you choose to believe). The bottom line was, I realized I had to go back and take a different approach to analyzing profiles to find a man that would actually be a good fit for me.

Let's take Bob, for instance. His profile read:

I'm not here for you to prove you found a better man than your ex or that you were always right. Do not put restrictions on my life because of what someone else did to you. I'm sure she's having fun, so I'm going to do the same.

When you combined his pictures with his bio questions and profile, Bob was gorgeous with sandy blonde hair and hazel eyes. He had muscles and towered over most at 6'4". Further, he didn't smoke, identified as a Christian, and liked to travel. I had to quell my kiddie-pool side and see what was really there – Bob had some issues. I had to read the profile several times before I really comprehended the message. At first, I thought he put the wrong pronoun because he is addressing a potential date in the first two sentences; however, upon seeing what was really there, it became clear he is talking about his ex in the third sentence. He wants to get even – his ex is having fun, and he's going to do the same.

If he were over her, if he wasn't angry or bitter about their split, she wouldn't be worth mentioning. In my opinion, Bob was looking for someone to be a distraction while he dealt with pain and even worse emotions. Bob seemed downright angry. For someone who was looking to find her soul mate, this would be a mismatch from the beginning simply because we would be at such different places from the get go with much different end goals. I didn't respond to Bob's wink.

About the time I dedicated myself to a deeper vetting process, I got a message from another man, Jack, who surfs the beach closest to me, which is still over three hours away. From his pictures, it's easy to see he's active and playful – and cute! His profile read:

Hey, ladies! I'm laid back and love the outdoors! Mountains, beaches, and rivers are my go-to spots. I'm always ready for an adventure – the Caribbean, island hopping, and cruising are things I love to do. I like to surf and play guitar as well. Looking for someone to just relax with who has no agenda.

Like Bob, Jack's bio pointed to the fact he was a non-smoker and a Christian. In one of his pictures, he looked like an older version of Brody surfing in *Point Break*. The kiddie pool was smitten, but my new commitment to better vetting set off the alarm bells. "No agenda" most likely meant he wasn't looking for a long-term commitment or even a commitment at all.
Still, I decided it wouldn't hurt to talk to Jack as long as I had no expectations of a real relationship. Sure enough, it didn't. I enjoyed conversing with this spirited islander, and he even promised to teach me to surf when the weather warmed up. I shared with my daughter that I might have to add surfing to the bucket list.

Jilly, by the way, loves this old television show called *Monk* about a neurotic ex-detective who helps the police solve crimes as a consultant. In fact, we had recently been binge watching Seasons 1-8 that we purchased from Vudu. It's quirky and the plots are predictable, but it is good family entertainment and quality acting; Tony Shalhoub won three Emmy's for Outstanding Lead Actor in a Comedy Series three out of the eight years it ran.

Anyway, each episode has a title, and they are all patterned like this, "Mr. Monk and the...." or "Mr. Monk goes to..." etc. So it might be, "Mr. Monk and the Red Herring" or "Mr. Monk Goes to the Circus."

So when I told Jilly about Jack who offered to teach me to surf, Jilly said, "Mom, we could write a series based on your dates."

Then she started listing, "Mom and the Surfer Dude," "Mom and the Preacher," etc., mimicking the way Monk episodes are titled, and I laughingly joined in, "Mom and the Inmate" and "Mom and the Fisherman." My dating life had been reduced from a quest to find a soul mate to a comedy series!

34
#grrrmondays

I had to get more serious about this online dating if I was to be successful, so I set my sites on Doug:

> Hi, I'm Doug – 6'2" with green eyes. I've raised my children who now attend college and I'm ready to spend some time on myself. Previously, working and taking care of my children has not left me much time for anything else, and I'm ready to make a change and find a nice lady to share new experiences with. I like all kinds of music and enjoy a variety of activities, including water sports. I'm active and healthy. I'm drama free and low maintenance, and I'm looking for a woman who is the same. I am well-read, and I can cook. If you're interested, I'd love to get to know you and see if we would be a good fit.

With my new vetting in place, Doug's profile didn't set off any alarm bells. After we communicated briefly, we went to see a movie and settled on a comedy.

When I wasn't on a date or with girlfriends, my movie-going partner of choice was Alex. We liked the same type of movies, which really included just about every genre, and we always had the best post-viewing discussions and analysis of what we had just watched. A few years prior to my date with Doug, Alex and I had gone to see *Ted 2*.

I knew it would have some lewd jokes, but it was even more base than I expected – and funnier than I imagined! It was one of those movies where I laughed so hard I couldn't catch my breath. (I mean this literally as I was dealing with the residual effects of "Respiratory Airway Disease" – which is a fancy way to say unconfirmed asthma – at the time.)

My favorite line in the movie was "F. Scott Fitzgerald? Why would you want to screw Scott Fitzgerald?"

It is so indicative of our slang and where our mindset is collectively anymore. It reminded me of the t-shirt I had seen once in an art gallery: "OMG! WTF has happened to the English language?" In my years of teaching English and dealing with slang, texting, and oratory laziness, I get it – and that shirt and the movie caused me to literally lol!!

The show was witty, chocked full of allusions. My favorite was when homage was paid to the *Breakfast Club*, with a recreation of a bit of the dance montage to "We Are Not Alone." It makes sense because *Ted 2* has a political message – the same as *Breakfast Club* – we are not so different.

Then there's Liam Neeson's cameo that references his *Taken* persona. He's buying *Trix*, a cereal that's just for kids – and Neeson wants the cashier to fully understand he is NOT a kid and is buying the cereal anyway; he worries there will be consequences. Again, I laughed so hard I could barely breathe.

I also enjoyed the mimicked scene from *Jurassic Park* when Dr. Grant first sees the living dinosaurs, but Ellie is preoccupied with a plant. He reaches down while she's yapping and without a sound turns her head to what (for a paleontologist) is the Holy Grail.

For the characters of *Ted 2*, their rapture is not quite so noble – a cash crop of top-shelf marijuana! But my point is this, an interesting phenomenon in the uncrowded theater that afternoon was the absence of laughter. Alex and I were at times the only ones cracking up in response to some extremely clever dialogue and spot-on allusions. This happens many times when we see movies, and it is probably the foremost reason why I enjoy watching movies with him more so than with most other people. Doug was a gentleman and obviously intelligent, but the entire time we were watching the movie, he never laughed – and I did frequently. Even though Doug was nice, I couldn't imagine spending my life with someone who had no sense of humor and couldn't see the lighter side of things. That night, I mentally added him to my one-and-done list.

By the way, after seeing *Ted 2*, I completely reframed Mondays. Anytime I'm having a-not-so-great Monday, I think of the scene where a rack of sperm samples spilled all over one of the characters; and his friend, instead of helping him up, first takes a picture for Instagram and tags it #grrrmondays. It's funny because it reflects life as we now know it, and I have a few hilarious snapshots of my friends to prove it. Oh, and it turned out I didn't have asthma either – just a really bad reaction to something in the air.

35
The Alibi

At this point, I could not decide if I really was a serial dater, if I was just too picky, or if all the men I could possibly connect with just somehow managed to stay married or stay away from dating websites. I wondered if I shouldn't just follow my dad's advice: "Keri, if God wants you to meet someone, he will send them to you."

I've always thought of myself as practical. When I'm sick enough to need medication, I go to the doctor even though I know God is capable of healing me. I believe God expects us to use the brains he equipped us with. With that in mind, I rationalized if I wanted a relationship, I should seek it out in the most logical fashion I could imagine. In spite of my lack of success, I still felt like online dating was the best way to meet men. My tenacity intact, I responded to a message from Phillip; it would be my most bizarre experience yet.

Do you ever wonder what makes us afraid? Is it our thin-slicing warning us a situation has a potential for disaster? And what's the real difference between fear and phobia? I guess fear is a reaction to imminent danger, and a phobia is anxiety related to a perceived threat or future threat or maybe even a non-existent threat. Anyway, I always challenge myself to face my fears, and one of the times I took the chance to do that was when Alex and I hiked Balcony House in Mesa Verde. I had taken this tour before when my daughter was younger, but I wanted to experience it without parental worries and distractions. So going with just

Alex made the experience altogether new for me.

I have known since I talked Alex into rock climbing at an indoor facility many summers ago he had a slight fear of heights, but I really wasn't aware of how strongly he battled his acrophobia until the Mesa Verde trip. To his credit, he knew for a couple of hours that he would be facing a thirty-two-foot ladder leaning on the face of a cliff; and likewise, I knew I would be crawling through a tunnel that the guide described as about the same width as the brim of his hat. Claustrophobia is my pet fear.

He got to go first. The ladder came early in the hike – and seeing it at the site is much different than viewing the small replica in the Visitor's Center. Right before we made the climb, I touched the palm of his hand. The sweat told me his fear was not an act. I had done Balcony House before, and in my opinion, the climb out has much greater exposure than the ladder, but I did not mention that to him. I know that when engaged in any kind of battle, especially a mental one, it is easier to focus on one obstacle at a time. I climbed the wide ladder beside him, thinking if he started to let his fear get the better of him, I could possibly be a voice of encouragement. But he did great; and had I not known what I knew, I wouldn't have suspected the ladder was a challenge to him at all.

I took a picture of him in the room where we landed, and he was cheesing – proud he had conquered. I still had not mentioned how we were going to have to exit the place, but at that moment, it was my turn to feel anxiety. I knew that soon, the tunnel would present itself. I battled with myself silently: "I've done this before; it wasn't that big of a deal. I obviously survived." But I couldn't rid my brain of the image of the brim of our guide's hat. It seemed so small. I continued to let my anxiety get the best of me, "What if getting through the first time was a fluke? My family was with me last time. I knew there was no way my kids would have left me stuck on a cliff. Alex won't leave me stuck on a cliff either – I'm pretty sure." And the truth was, I really couldn't remember what the tunnel looked like from the last time I was in Mesa Verde with my kids or how big it was or how scary. I checked my own palms, extremely sweaty.

    The tunnel came and Alex encouraged me from behind, "You're going to be fine." I relaxed a little and began to see it really wasn't as small as I remembered or believed. Besides having to put weight on a scraped knee and crawl on my elbows, in fact, it wasn't bad at all. And it turns out my acrophobic friend never looked back at the skyline as he climbed out of Balcony House. If he had, he would have noticed that a fall from the exit could take you all the way off the cliff except for the wire mesh placed by the Park Service…just in case.

    I met Phillip at a quaint barbeque joint in the town he had recently moved to, and my palms were only a little bit sweaty. I was standing outside the restaurant when I saw a gorgeous, silver-haired man approaching. His smile was instantly disarming, and I returned it with a big smile of my own and a greeting. When he reached me, he towered over me even in my signature high-heeled boots. Bending down, he gave me a spontaneous hug, and I felt the tension of meeting someone new immediately flee my body.

    It was not normal for me to do this, but I told him I had to take a quick selfie of us to send to my kids so that they would know who I was with. Maybe there was some thin-slicing going on after all. He obliged. Before I met Phillip, I did my usual, not-so-thorough, background check. As far as I could tell from some online stalking, he was from Canada and hadn't lived in the US long. He seemed to have some estranged relatives scattered around the country, but it appeared he moved to Texas mostly detached from friends and family. He told me as much as well – that he came here for work and had only made a few friends. Hence, the need to meet someone online. Seemed legit. Right?

Phillip had insisted prior to meeting for our date that since the drive was a long one for me, he would put me up in a hotel that night. If we got along, he suggested we could meet again the next morning and spend the day together. I really didn't like the idea of a near stranger paying for my hotel room, but I agreed to the plan.

After eating some of the best barbeque in Texas and listening to some live music, we decided to go see a movie. He mentioned a couple of friends of his, specifically his co-worker and her boyfriend, were grilling that night and had invited us to come by, but he preferred to spend the time alone with me so that we could get to know each other. I agreed. It was late when we left the theater and drove back to my car, and he had me follow him to a hotel he had obviously picked out in advance.

The town he lived in was quite large and had numerous hotels to choose from, so why he picked one across town from where he lived and where we enjoyed our entertainment that evening didn't make much sense. It turned out to be a nice motel instead of a hotel. As a woman, I prefer hotels because you don't enter the room from the street, and that gives me a little stronger sense of security when I'm staying alone.

Anyway, he had this particular motel in mind, and since he was paying for it, I didn't protest. He parked his car out front of the motel, and I parked mine behind him and followed him in. He paid with his credit card and registered the room in his name. I noticed the motel was about average-priced for the area, maybe even a little higher than average, and it registered in the back of my mind he didn't pick it out because it was the cheapest.

We went back outside, and I followed him around to the room, which was in the very back of the motel, in our respective cars. He carried my luggage, a Vera Bradley tote bag and make-up case, to the room, and he came inside briefly, closing the door behind him. He asked if he could pick me up around 9:00 the next morning, and I readily said he could. The evening had been fun – lots of conversation and laughing. I was hoping I might finally be making a connection.

The next morning, he picked me up at the motel a little after 9:00. It was a typically warm autumn weekend in Texas, and we were able to wear shorts and t-shirts and head out for the day. Phillip had been a hockey player in his younger days and still played on an adult coed league. He had a game that afternoon, and I was excited to be a spectator and cheer him on. Before the game, we grabbed some lunch, and he casually commented that the co-worker's boyfriend who had invited us to dinner only yesterday had died during the night. I was immediately concerned. He didn't have many friends in Texas, and one had just died!

I offered to leave at once so that he could go be with his co-worker or grieve or whatever, but he assured me he was fine and there was no reason for me to go home and he was going to play hockey regardless. So I accompanied him to the game and our easy conversation and laughter continued throughout the day.

I was impressed with his prowess on the ice. At fifty-two, he could still skate as well as the thirty- and forty-year-olds that were on his team. At one time, he skated to the edge of the rink where I was sitting, winked at me, and continued playing. He was agile and quick and scored two goals for his team. I made a mental note that I needed to learn the rules of hockey.

We decided on a sports bar for a dinner locale and started watching Game 4 of the World Series. The score would remain tied at zero until the bottom of the sixth when the Dodgers in their own stadium would go up, 4-0. However, the Sox would come back and score three runs in the seventh, one in the eighth, and five in the ninth to ultimately win the game, 9-6. While we shared Cajun shrimp and blueberry mojitos, I looked into the onyx eyes of the man next to me. I felt blessed to have stumbled upon a kindred sports enthusiast who fulfilled my kiddie-pool wish list to boot. Again, it was late, but this time I insisted on not only paying for my hotel room but choosing the location as well. Following a similar pattern to the night before, he carried my luggage to my room and came inside. We sat and talked for a few more minutes before he kissed me good-bye and asked if he could see me the next day before I left for home. It was a polite, sweet kiss – not passionate and without tongue. I was a little surprised since I considered it our second date.

The next morning, I was on the phone with Darla before Phillip arrived. She told me we should go to church because there was a Calvary Chapel in Phillip's town. I told her that would have been a good idea, but we had already missed the service time. She laughed and asked me what time I thought it was. It turned out the clock on the nightstand was set more than an hour ahead, and I had actually crawled out of bed, gotten dress, and called Phillip to come meet me pretty early, thinking it was later. When he arrived in shorts, flip flops, and a baseball cap, I suggested we go to church. He was flabbergasted that I would even consider darkening the doors of a church in our casual attire, but I assured him neither God nor the parishioners at this non-denominational church cared about how we were dressed. It was just a good day to worship the Lord. He acquiesced and accompanied me to join the small congregation that met in a downtown strip mall. Afterward, we went and grabbed a bite to eat and took a walk in a local park before I left. He claimed he liked me a lot and couldn't wait until we would go out again.

The next week, he called and texted daily – multiple times a day. Every morning I awoke to a "good morning" text, which was followed by a mid-morning call. He would contact me again during his lunch break – either by texting or a short phone call. In the evenings we would talk for an hour or more on the phone, and I got a "good night" text or call right before he retired for the night.

It was almost too much. He seemed thrilled our previous "dates" (I counted it as three) had gone so well and claimed to look forward to future dates and getting to know me even better. He discussed how much he liked me and thought I was a wonderful person. He even discussed the friend's funeral which would follow a full week after the man's death, and I asked if his co-worker was doing okay. He said she was doing well, and he was helping her move her stuff out of the boyfriend's house.

The day of the funeral came and went, and I heard from him the following morning. He texted that he was going to a neighboring town to do some shopping with his roommates, and he would call me that evening. We talked about "hating" the time change that made it dark by six, and before he left, he texted, "You are fabulous." Exact words. And I never heard another word. Not one word.

At first, I was unconcerned. I figured he was tired from the activities of the past few days and had fallen asleep early. The next morning, I did not receive my usual text, and I found it strange, so I texted "Good morning," to which I never got a reply. When I didn't hear from him at lunch or after work, I checked his Facebook account, and there had been no activity. I started to wonder what could be the problem – perhaps his phone was lost or broken?

I left a message on "Messenger," which can be accessed from a computer, just in case he was having problems with his phone. I fully understood we barely knew each other, and perhaps he had decided he preferred someone else, so I tried to make it easy for him to tell me he had moved on if that were the case:

> *Okay, I'm officially a little worried. You've been touching base so regularly for the past few weeks that it doesn't seem like you not to respond. If for some reason you don't want to talk anymore that is fine, but please give me a heads up. Otherwise, I might have to track you down and check on your well-being.*

On the third day after no response to my texts or messages and no activity on Facebook, I actually got worried. I started thinking if this man had been in an accident at some point, I'd have no way to know. Being resourceful, I took the little bit of information I had about his co-worker and tracked her down at work. I knew it would be a strange phone call, "Sheila, you don't know me, but my name is Keri. We have a mutual friend, Phillip. And I know this is strange, but I'm just calling to check on him. Do you know if he's okay?"

She became obviously flustered, stuttered a little, but then replied, "Yeah, he's fine."

I continued, "Well, could I leave my name and number in case he's having problems with his phone?"

Her curt and shaky response was, "Yeah, okay." Now, this lady worked at an office in a position that dealt with the public every day, yet she was shaken by my simple request to leave my number. Something felt very off. My thin-slicing was finally kicking in. Over the next few weeks, I never heard from Phillip, but I did some online snooping and found out Sheila had taken and posted a "What's your personality type?" quiz the day after her boyfriend died. Phillip had responded with a heart emoji. A few days after that she posted a picture of the two of them in an obvious couple's pose.

According to Occam's razor, also known as the law of parsimony, the simplest solution is the most likely solution. Most likely Sheila and Phillip already had a thing for each other, and when her boyfriend died, they simply had the opportunity to be together. I had been ghosted.

However, I couldn't help but wonder about a

few things. I imagined this scenario: Sheila and Phillip decided to get rid of her boyfriend. Maybe she was his life insurance beneficiary or something, and they needed him gone. Phillip decided to off him in a way that doesn't look like murder – maybe poison or smothering or something – but he wanted to have an alibi just in case anyone got suspicious.

He roped in a girl from out of town. Talked to her for several weeks, softening her so she'd let her guard down. He invited her to his town for an evening date, suggesting she stay overnight and he would pay for the hotel. Then he checked out various motels and found one that suited his need – security camera in the front office, but room in the back away from cameras. He made sure to be charming and on his best game so she would stay and go out again the next day. He even put a little gel in his hair to give it that slightly spiked, messy-sexy look. He checked her into the motel that night and then paid the boyfriend a visit. If anyone asked, he was on camera checking into a hotel with a blonde woman. His credit card backed that up. He continued to call and text her numerous times over the next seven days and pretended to remain interested until one week later – the day after the funeral – at which point the body was in the ground, and it seemed that all suspicion of foul play was buried as well. I've been a lot of things in this imperfect online dating journey, but wondering if I was someone's alibi took failing to a whole new level!

When I joked with Jilly about my theory, the little savant had an interesting observation. She said, "Mom, I notice when you describe Phillip, it is all about the smoldering eyes and gorgeous hair. Did you just pick him because he appealed to your kiddie pool?" I

185

answered with a chuckle. She finished, "Mom, you're drowning in your kiddie pool!"

36
Prolepsis

There are many dating websites out there, and many specialize in a particular audience so that like-minded people can find one another. Based on my experiences at this point in the journey, I had some ideas for a few more: *stillmarried.com, stalkertendencies.com, ineedanalibi.com*. Incredibly, at four years of trial and error, I was still no better at online dating than I was when I first started.

I put scrutinizing through profiles and beginning initial conversations with a few online potentials on hold so that I could spend the weekend doing something that would nurture the soul. It had been a while since Alex and I had talked, and I craved his perspective and company. We decided to wander around Cowtown, and by happenstance, landed in the Fort Worth Cultural District at the Museum of Modern Art.

The featured exhibit was "The Octopus Eats Its Own Leg," an extensive collection of the work of Japanese artist Takashi Murakami. Murakami is known for dabbling both in artistic expression and commercial products. The art was on display; the trinkets were on sale in the gift shop. It was an interesting juxtaposition. I knew enough about octopuses in captivity to know that if they become bored or stressed, they sometimes chew off their own appendages. It's called autophagy and seems like a legit reaction to being held captive in an aquarium to me.

Part of the fun of going to an art gallery with Alex – and we have been to several – is just enjoying the dialogue we will invariably exchange or the mental games we will play. For instance, a couple of years back during our time in Durango, we walked into a small unassuming gallery that boasted of independent artists, and we met Maureen May. It turned out the artist and Alex both grew up in Chicago. I listened to their comparative stories while I rummaged through some prints. Alex told the artist he had grown up in the same neighborhood as George Halas. That was news to me, but it now made sense as to why Alex used that moniker in his email address, and I wondered silently if he realized after years of sending correspondence to "ghalas," it is part of how I identify him. In some weird way, in fact, he is resonant of the caricature – Chicago Bears, sidewalks, and hot dogs. I recalled a poem I had once written about Chicago's hues.

"Which one speaks to me?" I asked silently as I took in the abstract images and read the corresponding titles. And I flipped to one with just a touch of lapis – blues my Chicago poem danced in my head:

> *Peering from a bench on the Southside*
> *Into a rundown building door*
> *Propped open to reveal*
> *Blues that weren't there before...*

And as I read the title of the print, *Prolepsis*, I remembered it was a literary term. I searched my brain, "What was that definition I taught my AP students many years ago?"

And it vaguely came to me, "A future event is prefigured, suggested, anticipated?" That was why I was in Durango in the first place – putting the past behind me and anticipating my new unmarried life. I quickly Googled the term to be sure I was remembering correctly. I saw "anticipation" on the screen and knew that I was right.

Since the beginning of my friendship with Alex, he had always accused me of "pre-feeling." An informal term he used to describe my insistence that I knew in advance how I would feel if this happened or that happened. I chuckled about my propensity for pre-feeling – wasn't that a form of anticipation? I decided to play a game with Alex. Leaving the artwork in its place in the pile, I asked him to search through the thirty or so pieces and pick out the one that appealed to me. I was also playing a game with myself: if he picked the blue-hued *Prolepsis*, I would buy it. What were the odds – about thirty to one? He had been busy getting to know the artist and was not paying attention to what I was doing at all.

Upon being challenged, he flipped through the square images, and without hesitation selected the very spot beneath which reposed the corpse of the victim! Really? How? My first thought was I had been duped. Either he had seen me lingering with this print or knew I had Googled the title.

I reminded him of a pact we had made long before in our friendship: although it is not necessary to reveal everything, we must never lie to one another. He maintained he had no prior knowledge of my selection. He even made reference to thin-slicing. He was the one who suggested I read *Blink* in the first place.

A hand-printed message from the artist and a

fist bump later, I was the proud, albeit perplexed, owner of the only existing copy of Maureen May's *Prolepsis*, which now sits in a museum-quality glass frame on my piano.

But at this exhibit, it was Murakami's work that had my attention – a hodgepodge of paintings, murals, and sculptures on a grand scale. Several of the pieces stand over fourteen-feet tall. And true to the anime it mimics, the colors in all of it are vivid and loud, and the large murals are a frenzy of activity. I tried to decipher exactly what was going on and was assaulted by the contradiction of sculptures that bordered pornographic and murals of child-like creatures and upbeat color mixed with images of skulls and demons. It is easy to see without reading the background of Murakami that he's making political statements – at least one concerning Japan's past – the bombing of Hiroshima and Nagasaki. If you do happen to look him up, you will discover the artist's mother had witnessed the destruction of the latter.

As we meandered through the exhibits, we took photos and discussed our impressions. At one point, we sat in front of a large blue curtain that sported a couple of numerals representing the artist's birthday. Nothing else. Yes, it was a piece in the exhibit. However, what I found more interesting at that moment (more interesting than the fact that a plain blue curtain was considered art) was the best friend who sat beside me. The museum was just an aside. I needed Alex's perspective. Since the divorce, he had consistently pushed me to stay the course and remain true to myself. He was the self-proclaimed "simple" man who showed up to a lunch date with pencils and paper to prove to me I could draw. In that same lesson, when I messed up, he said, "You know it's okay to erase, right?"

So much had changed in my life I felt like surely somewhere along the line I had jumped track and missed my correct destination. Nothing was going as planned and my striving was exhausting. Alex was always the antidote for self-pity; he would recap my blessings and remind me to just enjoy the journey and wait on God. He would tell me to stop overthinking and to stop pre-feeling and just be in the moment. I recalled a poster he had always displayed in his classroom – the word "whining," circled and crossed out with a diagonal line, the international symbol for "no." No whining.

The final climactic exhibit that day was the octopus itself, a large conceptual sculpture that looked like it had been covered in slick graffiti. In spite of the audacity and brilliance of the art, I was much more moved by the man with whom I shared it. And I calmly accepted his sage advice, "It's all good."

After I went out with Phillip and saw it from the perspective of hindsight, my daughter asked me, "Mom, were you ever in any real danger?"

I told her the truth, "Either I was in absolutely no danger at all, and my encounter with Phillip was entirely harmless, or I was in an extremely dangerous situation and unwittingly and unnecessarily put myself at risk." If I looked back on it, I could have been hit over the head and pushed into that hotel room. While I had covered my basis by letting people know who I was with, I had done little to actually protect myself during the date. Now, let's be honest, I'm from Texas. I bought the gun in the parking lot, remember? Strictly speaking to the ladies, however, you have to be able to access that gun quickly, or it does you no good. So while I may have been packing, I wasn't packing well that night if I'm completely honest. We'll just leave it at that. I want to be clear though: I had an abundance of fun those three days I hung out with Phillip. He was a hoot! So while I was still failing miserably at finding my soul mate, I was having a fabulous time in the process, not to mention I had made several new friends. Alex was right. It was all good – even when it wasn't!

Let me explain – and if you've found yourself single after a long marriage, you might agree. If my daughter is not with me, which is half the time, I no longer have to worry about what everyone is going to eat at night, who's going to cook, or even if there's food in the house. If I want I can have a bowl of cereal for dinner, which is one of my favorite things to do. Or I can have a pizza delivered, or I can go out with a friend and catch a bite, or I can just not eat anything at all. That's the beauty of single life. I don't have to do much advanced planning for just about anything.

And when my daughter is with her dad, I can also take off at a moment's notice and head out of town, visit my parents or grandkids, take a girls' trip, or do whatever I like; and there's no one else's schedule to worry about. I don't have to agree with a spouse about how money is spent or how the house will get decorated or for whom we will buy Christmas presents or any of those things healthy couples would discuss and come to consensus. There is something to be said for the independence of a single adult.

But there's also something to be said for sharing your life with someone who makes it brighter. I am still a romantic at heart and believe two people can create a synergetic situation that generates something greater than the two of them have apart from one another. My parents are living proof. So in spite of the failures and risk, I still believe my soul mate is out there.

37
Outhouses and Other Necessities

Back when my heart was in Leavenworth, I had written to John:

> A while back, I caught a piece about the Yanomami Indians of the Amazon. Instead of the usual anthropological look, a group of five artists had created an exhibition about the Yanomami. One of the artists was a "sound" artist. He recorded various sounds of the rain forests and indigenous animals, but more interesting were the mutterings of a tribal holy man. The artist explained that in the Yanomami language, they have attached meanings to animal sounds. For instance, (although this is not correctly paired) a monkey's squeal might mean a woman gave birth.
> Anyway, I found this completely fascinating. I thought about our culture and decided to a much lesser degree we have some similar associations with onomatopoeic words. A "meow" for instance, might signal a come hither mood if the intonation is low, the word drawn out into several syllables, and the emphasis placed on the "ow." The same sound, however, abbreviated, sharp, with the emphasis on the "me" conveys recognition of a bitchy statement.
> The holy man, however, seemed to hear the animal sounds more clearly and relate them more exactly. The perfect mimicry would, of course, be useful in hunting and other survival skills, but to

adopt them into your language, with meaning specific to the human tribe, was something I had not previously considered.

I've often been curious about animal communication, especially dolphin communication, which I did a brief study on in undergraduate school. Dolphins mimic sounds, like helicopters and birds. I'm wondering what meaning, if any, they attach to these sounds. There's no real point to anything I'm relating, except we've talked about your desire to backpack in the jungles of the world. After the story of the Yanomami, if I were to backpack in the jungle with you, I might listen differently.

What is peculiar about that letter was I was entertaining the idea of actually backpacking in the jungle with John. Let's unpack that for just a moment. I was considering trekking into terrain chock full of all sorts of crawly things while carrying on my back every single item I would need for the undertaking. Every piece of bedding, every toiletry, every item of clothing, every item for survival, every thing I would eat or drink – all of it would have to fit. I could only imagine how much this thing would weigh – even if I only brought one pair of heels and my smallest Kuerig. Not only was the heavy load a problem, but I would be sleeping on the ground and sharing it with any jungle inhabitant that felt the urge to crawl in and cuddle up beside me in the pitch dark.

Now I should tell you I once slept with a snake, but it was our ball python Lucy, and we were friends (or at the very least acquaintences), and it was out of necessity. An icestorm hit the town I lived in, and our electricity was knocked out for days. We had an electric central-heating system and no back-up generator. We could snuggle under blankets at night to keep warm, but our tropical pet snake's heating rock was rendered useless. To keep her from literally freezing to death, I got in a sleeping bag, zipped it up, and put Lucy inside with me so that my body heat would keep her warm. While she was cold, this idea worked. But when she got her temperature back up, she became very active and crawled all over and around me in that sleeping bag. Suffice it to say, I didn't get much sleep. By the way, my dad has always been a little suspicious of my snake handling, "Keri, there's something unnatural about a woman that likes snakes." I'm pretty sure that's because of his Baptist upbringing and Eve allowing herself to be tempted by the serpent. My issue is more with Adam. He's standing next to a naked woman and is tempted by a piece of fruit. What's up with that?

  In spite of having slept with Lucy, I had no desire to snooze with any other snakes or spiders or centipedes or…well, let's just leave it at any jungle inhabitants whatsoever. Besides what might decide to slither into camp, I was also a bit concerned about the creatures in the jungle who could possibly want to suck my blood. I'm not exaggerating that the mosqitos are cause for a transfusion and the leeches are just gross. And we haven't even discussed those jungle animals that are large enough to actually be inclined to consume all of me – versus just suck a little blood.

  Then there's this tricky little thing called personal hygiene. Assuming I was able to carry enough food and water for consumption, what goes in must come out. I have actually had the good fortune of using a double-decker outhouse while camping in

Colorado, where you can sit on a piece of wood with a hole that plunges down to who knows where while your neighbor sits above you and simultaneously drops down his or her excrement in a tube that is conveniently located behind your head. As far as I'm concerned, that is the most extreme potty game I ever want to play. Hugging a tree in a jungle teeming with creepy crawlers while hoping the guy of your dreams waits downwind just does not sound like a good bonding activity to me. Further, and this is important for you ladies to know, you should not shave in the jungle because if you nick yourself, a small cut can turn into a nasty infection. I'm just trying to picture myself waxing on a fallen log – or worse sporting a couple week's worth of growth in all those places ladies don't like to have hair. Now do you understand the fact I even considered going backpacking in the jungle with this man at all was extraordinary?

I think I just wanted to test the theory to see if I'd get carried instead of left behind. Turns out, I didn't need to go all the way to the jungle to find out. I got left behind while he was still in Leavenworth, or so I thought.

John came up for parole a second time, and again the Army made it clear that unless he confessed to the crimes he was convicted of he wasn't getting out. The things that are usually considered during a parole hearing – good behavior, recidivism, viable employment – were all moot points as far as the Army was concerned. It was now a matter of principle for both parties – the Army couldn't risk releasing a decorated non-commissioned officer who never admitted guilt, and John would never admit to something he didn't do. It was a standoff.

But a fellow veteran refused to give up and finally got a face-to-face audience with the President – a president who supported the plight of the soldier on the ground over the bureacrat sitting behind the desk. A President with the power of the pardon. It was a long shot, but for John, it was the most hopeful he had been in his nearly decade of imprisonment.

I was more than a little surprised when he called me and asked, "Keri, if I get out of here, and if you're not married yet, will you go to dinner with me?"

The phone call made me restless, and I had to do something with myself other than get lost in my head, so I pulled out my pencils and decided to draw. I always liked drawing the human form, and I had John on my mind; so I decided to draw the nude backside of a seated male. It took a moment for me to tap into that spot on the right side that would see what was really there. Finally, I did, and the form begin to emerge. When I was almost done, my pencil slipped, and I made a stray mark.

A little upset with myself, I picked up the eraser, and it hit me. Why do we perceive erasing as bad? That somehow we are lessened if we have to erase – perhaps erase something in the past – a mistake, a painful memory? Yet erasing is a part of the process in any work of art – written, drawn or lived. When we erase a stray mark – a line that is in the wrong place, a word that detracts from the unity of the whole, a mistake we made in life – isn't it to improve on the totality? The darker the original mark, the harder erasing may become; and in actuality, there is likely a trace of what we tried to remove, but that trace lightens, smudges, and blends to become masked in the new product.

At that moment I had an epiphany: erasing shouldn't be understated or devalued. Life often calls for us to purge a little of the past, remove the unhealthy stray marks or the words that lessen the whole. And when we take the time to erase – through forgiveness, releasing, forgetting, even moving forward – only a hint is left, and it fades and mixes into a new picture so subtly that even the one who erased it may forget it was there at all. Erasing does not make one less of an artist…or less of a person. It is necessary to complete any *magnum opus*, especially the one we call life.

With each and every encounter in my dating journey, I had added to the canvas and erased when necessary. I am still drawing…and erasing. I have no idea what the final destination will be, but the journey is fabulous. And while my profile is still online out there in dating wonderland, I think I'll just be still and keep that dinner date card John offered open for now…just in case.

Epilogue:
Failing A Hero: The Story of John E. Hatley's Shocking Conviction and Incarceration

April 16, 2019, marked ten years that an American soldier has been incarcerated for a crime that he did not commit.

John E. Hatley is a highly-decorated 20-year combat veteran and Army Ranger, who is now incarcerated in the United States Disciplinary Barracks at Leavenworth for the premeditated murder of four men of Middle Eastern descent. If it seems like an open and shut case, it is anything but.

In April 2009, Hatley was sentenced to life. His sentence was subsequently reduced to 40 years and then, to 25 years. Hatley is serving that sentence in the USDB at Fort Leavenworth, Kansas. **There is just one problem: there were no murders.**

Hatley has maintained his innocence since the beginning and has refused to waiver and compromise his honor. Hatley's plight began during a climate of "punishing US soldiers" (e.g. the "Leavenworth 10") as a reaction to political opposition to the American presence in the Middle East and the accusations of inhumane treatment of detainees in Guantanamo Bay at the hands of the US Army. In the wake of the backlash, the Army upper echelon engaged in an effort to "prove" that they held US soldiers to high standards of engagement and accountability for their actions. Unfortunately, this effort culminated in a witch-hunt-like frenzy that ultimately led to a myriad of questionable court-martials of soldiers who were simply carrying out their duties in combat situations and were not guilty of any wrongdoing. It also led to a climate of fear and finger-pointing within the ranks. Coupled with the anomaly of the military's incredibly high conviction rate in spite of a lack of evidence, this created fertile ground for the convictions of innocent soldiers.

Further, in this same climate, some mainstream media painted American soldiers as cold-blooded killers. Hatley was not only severely defamed by the media in general, but a well-known magazine featured an article about his case that fed the American public outright lies. Hatley wrote a detailed rebuttal, but it was not published by the magazine nor were the false statements retracted. Thus, if one is attempting to find factual information about the case, it has become impossible to sort through the misinformation without access to the record of trial, supporting documents, and direct interviews with the witnesses, including Hatley himself. Every detail put forth here is supported by all of these.

Hatley was convicted solely on the accusation of a soldier, Jesse Cunningham, whom he was in the process of bringing charges against, and the coerced and coached testimony of a handful of his men who were threatened with life in prison and never seeing their families again, and who were each being told the others were pointing the finger at them. With a court martial-conviction rate of almost 98%, these few accused soldiers – with the exception of Hatley – were not willing to take the chance to fight for the truth.

Sometime during March or April of 2007, a firefight occurred between First Sergeant Hatley's unit and a group of Iraqi fighters. Hatley and his men chased the insurgents to a house about four blocks away from the initial firefight. The house was occupied by women and children who said they were the men's wives and children. The men were taken into custody and a large cache of weapons and ammunition was recovered. However, as per the stringent policies pertaining to detaining enemy combatants, there was not enough evidence to detain the insurgents. This was a routine scenario for American soldiers, and First Sergeant Hatley made the decision to take the five detained prisoners to the outskirts of their sector and release them, which, according to Hatley, they did without incident.

Ten months after this event, Cunningham was facing two charges of striking a fellow NCO and one charge of threatening an officer with great bodily harm. Cunningham asked his attorney to take an offer of a deal to the Criminal Investigation Division (CID) of the Army offering information on a homicide in exchange for immunity. Immunity was denied, but the attorney had already given CID Cunningham's statement. At this point, Cunningham did not cooperate with CID, but they decided to proceed with the investigation by bringing in a different soldier in the unit they had determined to be easily manipulated. This soldier wore a wire for three to four weeks in an attempt to gather incriminating information; however, no incriminating information was obtained. It stands to reason that CID would have coached this man on how to engage others in a particular discussion, yet they got nothing.

Next, CID brought all of the men in the unit in for questioning. Those who had been part of the patrol were interrogated for days using offers of reduced sentences or immunity and threats of life in prison (including the effects on their families). They were told others had incriminated them.

Eventually, all of the men except Hatley made pretrial or post-trial agreements to plead guilty. This is understandable considering the Army has a conviction rate of nearly 98% and the full weight of the US government behind them. Hatley was offered the same deal if he would roll over on his superior, but Hatley would neither plead guilty to something he didn't do or falsely implicate someone else.

There was not a single shred of physical or forensic evidence against Hatley or his co-accused, Sergeant First Class Joseph P. Mayo and Sergeant Michael Leahy. A seven-man Army diving team searched the canal where Cunningham said four men were executed and the bodies were supposedly dumped. They found nothing. According to CID, no bodies, no items of clothing, no personal belongings, no bone fragments, no bullets, or no casings were found. CID had one of the soldiers take them to the house where the five enemy fighters had been apprehended to interview the family members of the supposed victims. All of them said they knew of no one missing or dead. No names were obtained. Further, CID interviewed neighbors from the surrounding areas who said no one was missing from the neighborhood. Also, CID interviewed the farmer on whose land the canal is located where the alleged bodies were dumped. The farmer said he had zero knowledge of any bodies being dumped or anyone being murdered in that area. **None of this was disputed, and, remarkably, the case went to trial with no victims being identified.**

According to Hatley and several others on the patrol that day, five men – not four – were taken into custody and released. The prosecutors were aware that "witnesses" could not agree on how many people were allegedly executed, but this did not deter them in seeking a conviction. At his trial, Hatley told his lawyer that five men were taken into custody, and his lawyer told him not to bring it up or they might just charge him with another murder. The testimonies at trial included several key points of contradiction when it came to the alleged execution, including how many men were captured and supposedly shot, who fired shots and in what order, how many shots were fired, and where shots were placed. Further, testimony was accepted by one man who was known to have previously given a false statement to the CID, and some of the testimony contradicted the laws of physics. **This is important because Hatley was convicted solely on testimony, and that testimony was contradictory and inconsistent.**

Hatley, unaware at the time of the tactics used in a military court-martial, trusted his counsel implicitly. He said to his lawyer, "I'm putting my faith in you because this is your area of expertise. If we were in downtown Baghdad, I'd expect you to shut up and do as you're told because that's my area of expertise. That's why I plan on keeping my mouth shut and trusting you to get me through this."

His lawyers advised him not to testify on his own behalf. Further, they did not send independent investigators to the crime scene, which seemed unnecessary at the time because CID found no physical or forensic evidence and was unable to identify any victims. In hindsight, Hatley would learn that the military he had served without question for the past nineteen and a half years had no qualms about sacrificing him to further their own agenda. He would also learn that when accused by the military, he was, in essence, guilty until proven innocent, and neither he nor his legal counsel understood up front that the burden of proof was slanted against him.

The Uniform Code of Military Justice (UCMJ) is a broken and corrupt system that has imprisoned more than one innocent man. It is nothing like a civilian court. Little to no evidence is needed for a conviction. Hatley, and other American soldiers in similar situations, have no recourse for a retrial in a civil court in spite of their status as American citizens.

Further, the Deputy Assistant to the Army, Francine Blackmon, vetoed the parole board who had initially granted Hatley's parole in 2017. Guilt or innocence aside, Hatley has been a model prisoner since his incarceration. As evidenced in his parole packet, he has not only maintained his high standards of conduct and leadership, he has positively influenced the behavior of others within his pod and has been instrumental in changing the culture of it so that very few problems occur. Hatley has saved a life while incarcerated and has never been sent to isolation for disciplinary purposes. Further, he has been determined to be zero risk for recidivism and his parole packet included evidence of multiple job offers and strong family and community support for acclimating back into society. These are the requirements relevant to his request for parole.

In 2017, the Parole Board after thoroughly reviewing his packet and listening to the testimony of those who spoke on his behalf, including United States Congressman Bill Flores, agreed and voted to grant him parole. However, Francine Blackmon vetoed their decision citing the "heinous nature of the crime" as her reason for doing so. However, Blackmon was inconsistent with her own previous decisions and, therefore, had some other underlying motive for her actions. In 2015, Blackmon had approved the parole of the co-accused soldiers, Leahy and Mayo, who had been convicted with the same culpability as Hatley. Blackmon, in those two cases, supported the decision of the Board to grant parole and did not reverse based on "the heinous nature of the crime," but yet those two men served even less time in prison than Hatley. She set the precedent by granting their parole the very first time they came up for review. Even on the premise that a crime was committed, how was the crime less heinous for these two soldiers than for Hatley?

In 2018, the same board that granted Hatley parole the first time denied it on the basis that he is not taking responsibility for his actions. Doing so, they have, in essence, denied his right to maintain his innocence.

Hatley, a 50-year-old native Texan, with a longstanding combat and military career as a Paratrooper, Ranger, and Infantryman, has an impeccable record both in the military and the USDB – both before and after the supposed crime. His character has not changed; he is still the same highly-decorated non-commissioned officer who received numerous accolades for his honor, sacrifice and valor, including two Bronze Stars, an Army Commendation Medal for Valor, the Ranger Tab, and induction into the Audie Murphey Club, which is an honor reserved for men who demonstrate a myriad of leadership and character traits. Hatley has stated that nothing means more to him than his name and his honor and that he will sit in the USDB for the entirety of his sentence rather than confess to a crime he did not commit. In this regard, the Uniform Code of Military Justice, the United States Army, and the United States as a whole have failed to protect the constitutional rights and liberty of a soldier who has put his very life on the line to protect those same rights and liberties for all other US citizens.

Sources:
Record of Trial, US vs. MSgt. Hatley, John E. (2009) Clemency and Parole Packet and accompanying documentation, including Military Service Record, Confinement Record, Disciplinary Record, Clemency Consideration Criteria, Awards and Achievements; John E. Hatley (2017)

United American Patriots **https://www.uap.org/john-hatley-bio**

Personal Interviews and Correspondence, John E. Hatley (2016-2019)

Free John Hatley Website **http://freejohnhatley.com** (Rose Lipscomb, Webmaster, in conjunction w/John N. Maher, UAP Attorney)

Article reprinted from Criminal Justice Law International **http://criminaljusticelaw.org/?s=hatley**

Made in the USA
Lexington, KY
10 May 2019